Rumors of War

RUMORS OF WAR

A Moral and Theological Perspective on the Arms Race

Edited by C. A. Cesaretti
and Joseph T. Vitale

THE SEABURY PRESS · NEW YORK

For Barbara and J.D.R.

Note to the Reader
All biblical references are to the Revised Standard Version of the Bible. Old Testament Section, copyright © 1952; New Testament Section, First Edition, copyright © 1946; Second Edition © 1971 by Division of Christian Education of the National Council of Churches of Christ in the United States of America.

1982
The Seabury Press
815 Second Avenue
New York, N.Y. 10017

Library of Congress Cataloging in Publication Data

Main entry under title:
Rumors of War.
    1. Christianity and war.   I. Cesaretti, C.A.
II. Vitale, Joseph T.
BT736.2.R83   261.8'73   81-18400
ISBN 0-8164-2365-2   AACR2

Contents

"And you will hear of wars and rumors of wars;
see that you are not alarmed; for this must
take place, but the end is not yet."

(Matthew 24:6)

"We have to have armies! We have to have military
power! We have to have police forces, whether it's
in a great city or police in an international scale
to keep those madmen from taking over the world
and robbing the world of its liberties."

Billy Graham in 1965

"The people of the United States want peace. The
people of China want peace. The people of the Soviet
Union want peace. Why can't we have peace? We don't
realize the proliferation of these weapons and
the arms race of $400 billion that we're spending on
arms in the world — insanity, madness!"

Billy Graham in 1979

Foreword

Writing about *Moby Dick* in 1927, E. M. Forster stated: *"Moby Dick* is an easy book, so long as we read it as a yarn or an account of whaling interspersed with snatches of poetry. But as soon as we catch the song in it, it grows difficult and immensely important. The essential in *Moby Dick,* its prophetic song, flows athwart the action and the surface morality like an under-current. It lies outside words."

What Forster wrote about *Moby Dick* applies with precision to the arms race. Just as *Moby Dick* is not about ships and sailors and whales, the arms race is not about bombers and cruise missiles and submarines. What is common between the famous tale of the sea and the harsh reality of nuclear armaments is that what we *sense* about them matters so much more than anything we can say about them. There is a deep human connection between the destruction and waste of the arms race and that haunting scene at the end of *Moby Dick* when Starbuck cries out to Captain Ahab that it is not too late to desist: "Moby Dick seeks thee not. It is thou, thou, that madly seekest him!"

Rumors of War does not seek to tell the reader all about bombers, cruise missiles, or submarines. It is an attempt to create a learning environment in which the human tensions that exist within each of us are explored.

Rumors of War is about peace, security, justice, and preservation. It is about the global tensions found in each of us in microcosm. It attempts to bridge the gap between human emotions and the tumultuous rage of nations.

Moby Dick is a symbolic account of the conflict between man and his fate. Ahab loses his ship and his life — he fails to be master of his fate.

The accelerating arms race seems to be our living anew this ancient conflict. In the recesses of our hearts we intuit that we may lose our civilization — and our future — if we fail to be captains of our souls.

John Maury Allin

Introduction

Their names are legend: Alexander the Great, Hannibal, Julius Caesar, Attila, Napoleon, Wellington, Nelson, Rommel, Bradley, Patton, Zhukov.

The battles are history: Thermopylae, Salamis, Cannae, Waterloo, Trafalgar, Tobruk, The Coral Sea, Dien Bien Phu.

Out of the death and destruction of war have come a romantic tradition and myth. Out of the cavalry charge, the trumpet call, the crusade has been formed by the vocabulary of heroism, chivalry, and valor. Out of rape, pillage, and treachery has been built the illusion of self-sacrifice, duty, and justice.

Parish churches have been named after soldier saints. Stained-glass windows, wall plaques, and churchyard monuments recall and herald the deeds of faithful warriors. As Lesbia Scott wrote in her famous hymn for children:

> And one was a soldier, and one was a priest,
> and one was slain by a fierce wild beast;
> and there's not any reason — no, not the
> least — why I shouldn't be one too.

Politically, sociologically, and religiously, peace is alien to us.

It is difficult to hope for peace when there are rumors of war; when the glorification of the martial arts surrounds us; when language absorbs and sanitizes the vocabulary of battles; when history and literature provide a selective memory; when romantic accounts of wars fail to mention their root causes: pride, rapaciousness, the desire for land, food, resources, or sheer mastery.

It is difficult to work for peace when the military is associated with discipline and honor; when security is defined as "mutual assured destruction"; when political rhetoric creates a wonderland of opposites: armaments equal peace, international tension equals security, nuclear superiority equals freedom, peace equals defeat, peacemaker equals traitor.

It is difficult to pray for peace when the liturgies and hagiographies of religious communities naively evoke the imagery of armies, battles, swords, and shields; when places of worship and meditation are museums of armaments of the earthly powers and principalities.

It is difficult to truly understand peace because of evil, evil and its human manifestation: sin.

But hope, work, pray, and understand peace we must.

There are many who say that it is not the role of the church or the individual Christian to engage in a debate over the MX missile, or the M-1 tank, or the B-1 bomber. But this debate is really not about weapons at all — it is about human nature and human destiny. It is about the discrepancy between what we say and what we do.

The tension that Christians experience today over the arms race is not only the tension of our time, but the tension of the opposites, the paradoxes, found in the New Testament. For example, two statements of Jesus in the Gospels seem irreconcilably opposed: "All who take the sword shall die by the sword" (Matthew 26:53) and "There is no greater love than this, that a man should lay down his life for his friends" (John 15:13). How does one live with these sayings of Jesus when faced with armed conflict? If we define war as a way to protect our friends (say, in Western Europe) and take the sword to defend them, do we condemn ourselves by the sword? If we refuse to take the sword in defense of our friends, we seem to deny the greater love.

Historically and theologically, the Christian is caught in a moral bind in his view of war and, more especially, in the technological and nuclear war of today. Christianity has traditionally advanced two positions for the followers of the Prince of Peace: the crusade and the just war. These two attitudes are based on an ethic grounded in the will to implement in proper balance love, justice, the integrity of self, and the integrity of the other — even if that *other* is the enemy.

The task before the Christian, especially the moral leadership of the church, is to examine armed conflict in the light of these ground rules before identifying it as either a crusade or a just war. Aside from evaluating war as meeting the ethic of love, justice, and integrity, the Christian must also observe that its execution is commensurate with certain ideals. The amount of force in a war must not be more than is strictly necessary. The evils which the war creates must not be greater than the evils which it is designed to correct. Force must be discriminatory and must not be aimed at innocent people who are noncombatants or not directly engaged in the war effort. The war must be defensive in character; and the aim of the war must be to reestablish creative and friendly relations.

Today, Christians must be prepared to examine not only the justifiability of war but its conduct and preparation. A war must not become the attempt of one side to vanquish another by any means. If it does, that very fact makes it utterly unjust and immoral, *no matter how great the cause (or how righteous)*. When the means of war violate Christian ethics, that war is immoral and *must* be condemned and Christians *must* work for its immediate end.

These are vital questions because, since 1945, there has been a very real war going on: the arms race between the United States and the Soviet Union which has spread to other nations. Right now, the United States and the Soviet Union are arming themselves in an effort to vanquish the other *by any and all means* — a clear violation of the traditional Christian doctrine regarding war.

The current runaway arms race between the United States and the USSR is a very real *moral* question for all Christians and must be faced squarely. It will not quietly disappear. Like a cancer it will only grow with nontreatment and eventually it *will* kill us. Our nation, indeed almost every industrial nation of the world (including the USSR) is suffering from its deleterious effects. And yet our leaders call for more arms, larger and more deadly bombs, more expensive weapons systems. As our cities decay, as our youth goes unemployed, as the middle class suffers from an ever-increasing cost of living and a cutback in essential services, the Pentagon grows wealthier by the minute. Whether or not Christians wish to admit or recognize it, we are worshiping at the altar of a false god, a pagan idol: Mars, the god of war.

"Because of the nature of the Christian faith, we have an imperative obligation to pray and work for peace among men and nations." With those words the 1962 House of Bishops committed the Episcopal Church to put into practice the Christian mission of peacemaking. Today, there is a growing awareness in all churches that it is important, even mandatory, to address the "peace issue." In the nuclear age, with the sophisticated weaponry of mass destruction, a decision on the "justness" or "unjustness" of war would have to be limited to perhaps three minutes (the time it would take for an American or a Russian submarine-launched missile to reach its target). It is therefore imperative that such a decision be made in advance or not at all.

Rumors of War has been designed as a guide for adult discussion groups seeking to come to grips with the religious aspects — as well as many other dimensions — of the arms race. It was created as a tool for groups trying to understand this increasingly important "fact of life" in the last decades of the twentieth century.

In designing *Rumors of War*, we have attempted to use the approach favored by many contemporary Christian educators. In addition, the book takes its moral and ethical stance from *The Christian Moral Vision* by Earl Brill (volume seven of *The Church's Teaching Series*). It provides a framework of four study sessions (Peace, Security, Just War, Stewardship and Christian Responsibility) within which concerned adults may come to terms with what the arms race means to their country — and to themselves as individuals: economically, politically, and spiritually. The sessions provide alternative possibilities that will allow most groups to tailor the series closely to their personal and community needs. The three appendices provide a rich variety of supplementary reading material that has been integrated into the study sessions themselves. An extensive and carefully chosen list of books, articles, audiovisual materials, and organizations will lead the reader to even wider horizons.

In the dedication of the *War Requiem*, Benjamin Britten quotes Wilfred Owen, whose poetry comprises the libretto of this stirring testimony against war. Owen's verse was written on the battlefields of World War I, where he was killed just one week before the Armistice. Britten recalls Owen's well-known poetic manifesto: "My subject is War, and the pity of War. The Poetry is in the pity. . . . All a poet can do today is warn."

We hope *Rumors of War* can serve not only as a warning but as a plan of action. Encouraging words, contemplation, soul-searching, and prayer without subsequent action are meaningless in today's dangerous world situation. As William C. Frey writes in his essay in this book, "Prayer without action is blasphemous."

The arms race is a weight that every man, woman, and child is forced to carry. Perhaps someday·we may heed the scriptural call of Isaiah to "undo the heavy burden and let the oppressed go free" (58:6).

It is toward that end that this book is dedicated.

C. A. Cesaretti
Joseph T. Vitale

Notes on Organizing the Group

Rumors of War is a resource book for adults. It contains the structure for bible study; three appendices with personal and media perspectives; documents and statements by a number of religious, scientific, and volunteer agencies; a Glossary, and a detailed list of resources. All this is intended to supply the individual and the group, as well as the appointed or elected leader, with material for thought, discussion, further investigation, and personal commitment. A certain amount of the material is controversial — as are the issues they address — but the profit is in the grist for mature, enlightened dialogue.

The ideal length for the four sessions is an hour and a half to two hours. With careful planning and leadership, they may be held at the traditional Sunday morning adult education time, or as a midweek bible study and discussion series. Or, they may be held at a weekend parish conference, by a cluster of parishes in your area, or by an ecumenical study group.

This is not a series to drop in and out of, despite its flexibility and relative informality. There is an underlying assumption that the participants are committed to learning something about themselves as well as one of the world's most pressing problems. It may be helpful to underline the serious nature of the issue and the personal dimension by having each participant enter into a "contract" or "covenant" with the leader and with one another, sealing their commitment to the entire program.

In some instances it may be possible to have more than one group use this resource book. Each session may be tailored to meet the specific needs of the participants. Whatever the separate arrangements, serious consideration should be given to a sharing of learnings. This joint meeting may offer the opportunity for common worship.

Getting Started

Suggestions for the person or persons who will lead the sessions:

- Read *Rumors of War* in its entirety before you announce the series.
- Identify a number of people who can provide a nucleus for the discussion group or groups.
- Explore the time and date options and select those that meet the needs and resources available.
- Check with your parish library or local public library for the availability of resources listed in Appendix C. Arrange for a reserve section for supplementary reading.
- Arrange well in advance for audiovisual material or guest speakers.
- Have copies of *Rumors of War* available for purchase at the time of signing up for the program.
- Consult with those responsible for the liturgy, music, and education in your parish. They may have suggestions or may agree to incorporate resources into their area of expertise.
- Announce the program in every parish bulletin, leaflet, or mailing.
- Provide sign-up opportunities after worship services, coffee hours, or parish meetings. Follow up registrations with a personal call either by telephone or in person.
- Encourage each participant to read the Foreword, the Introduction, Appendices A and B, and any appropriate articles *before* the group meets for the first time.
- Have a preseries session to:
  - — discuss the series and issues raised
  - — read the Foreword and the Introduction
  - — assign a facilitator and observer for each session
  - — list all the aids you may need, for example: a 16mm movie projector and screen, *and* someone who knows how to operate the projector. An extra bulb for the projector? Extension cord?

Note: *Equipping God's People,* by Gary T. Evans and Richard E. Hayes (Seabury Press, 1979) is an excellent source for the basic concepts of adult education.

Rumors of War is a self-contained study guide comprising a wealth of data that includes opinion and primary sources. The leader should be well acquainted with these valuable aids to informed group discussion.

Appendix A brings together a series of personal statements, historical and contemporary, about war and peace. Appendix B is a collection of essays from the media. The leader will want to be fully acquainted with these appendices, noting the working relationship between them.

The Glossary provides a quick reference to terms frequently used in discussing the arms race.

The resource section contains a select bibliography, current audiovisuals, and short articles on the various aspects of the arms race. All the resources have been chosen for their availability and lucid, crisp style for the layperson. The selection also contains a listing of domestic organizations, groups, and agencies. This list is keyed to specific concerns and services. The resource section is designed to expand the horizon of the leader and motivated participants.

Preparing for the First Session
(Peace)

• Encourage each participant to read the appropriate selections in Appendices A and B—the articles by Pope John Paul II and William C. Frey on pages 60–67 and the article by Jerry Richardson on page 78.

Session 1

Peace

Bible Study and Discussion

Begin the session with the Bible and appropriate prayer. All of the sessions will begin with a reading from Scripture. The leader or a member of the group should begin the first session by reading aloud St. Matthew 10:34–42. It is a disturbingly provocative reading and a period of silent reflection may be helpful before beginning the discussion period.

St. Matthew 10:34–42

"Do not think that I have come to bring peace on earth; I have not come to bring peace, but a sword. For I have come to set a man against his father, and a daughter against her mother, and a daughter-in-law against her mother-in-law; and a man's foes will be those of his own household. He who loves father or mother more than me is not worthy of me; and he who loves son or daughter more than me is not worthy of me; and he who does not take his cross and follow me is not worthy of me. He who finds his life will lose it, and he who loses his life for my sake will find it.

He who receives you receives me, and he who receives me receives him who sent me. He who receives a prophet because he is a prophet shall receive a prophet's reward, and he who receives a righteous man because he is a righteous man shall receive a righteous man's reward. And whoever gives to one of these little ones even a cup of cold water because he is a disciple, truly, I say to you, he shall not lose his reward."

Talk about Matthew 10:34–42. These questions may help the group get started:

1. Do you think that Jesus is using figurative language?
2. *Compare* this passage with Luke 12:49–56, or Luke 22:35–38.
3. *Contrast* this passage with Matthew 26:51–56.

4. What kind of "divisions" does the sword bring? How? Why?

5. What is the difference between "peace" and "lethargy" or "complaisance"?

6. Do you agree with Cervantes (*Don Quixote,* pt. I, bk. IV, p. 10): "Let none presume to tell me that the pen is preferable to the sword."

7. Complete this sentence: Peace is . . .

Moving Along

The group has been asked to read the Foreword and Introduction to this book.

1. What does Bishop John Allin mean in the Foreword when he says that "the arms race is not about bombers, cruise missiles and submarines"?

2. After reading the article by Richard J. Barnet (page 71), list the points with which you agree and/or disagree.

3. What is the basic concept underlying "deterrence" as presented in George Kennan's article (page 25)? Don't forget to check all terms in the Glossary.

4. In his essay, (page 30) General MacArthur says that the outlawing of global war would "produce a wave of economic prosperity that would raise the world's standard of living beyond anything ever dreamed of by man." Discuss some worldwide (and domestic) problems that might be eliminated if the billions now spent on the arms race were turned to humanitarian uses. What would the face of peace look like?

5. Compare Wilfred Owen's poem quoted in the Introduction, with William Butler Yeats's "On Being Asked for a War Poem":

> I think it better that in times like these
> A poet's mouth be silent, for in truth
> We have no gift to set a statesman right;
> He has had enough of meddling who can please
> A young girl in the indolence of her youth,
> Or an old man upon a winter's night.

Preparing for the Next Session
(Security)

Start to discuss what the design and agenda for the next session ought to be.

• Encourage each participant to read the appropriate selections in Appendices A (pages 25–55) and B (pages 83–104).

• Look ahead to the suggested discussion questions in Session 2 and briefly focus the attention of the participant on the issues suggested.

• Suggest that the participants bring various translations of the Scripture for comparison, allowing the language to bring new insights.

Ending

• Read aloud: Micah 4:1–5
• Pause for silent meditation and reflection.
• Share personal prayers and intercessions.
• Read aloud:

O Lord our Governor, bless the leaders of our land,
that we may be a people at peace among ourselves
and a blessing to other nations of the earth.
Lord, keep this nation under your care.
To the President and members of the Cabinet,
to Governors of States, Mayors of Cities,
and to all in administrative authority, grant
wisdom and grace in the exercise of their duties.
Give grace to your servants, O Lord.
To Senators and Representatives, and those who
make our laws in States, Cities, and Towns, give
courage, wisdom, and foresight to provide for
the needs of all our people, and to fulfill our
obligations in the community of nations.
Give grace to your servants, O Lord.
To the Judges and officers of our Courts give
understanding and integrity, that human rights
may be safeguarded and justice served.
Give grace to your servants, O Lord.
And finally, teach our people to rely on your
strength and to accept their responsibilities
to their fellow citizens, that they may elect
trustworthy leaders and make wise decisions
for the well-being of our society; that we may
serve you faithfully in our generation and honor
your holy Name.
For yours is the kingdom, O Lord, and you are
exalted as head above all. Amen.

Say together:

> Lord, make us instruments of your peace.
> Where there is hatred, let us sow love;
> where there is injury, pardon; where there
> is discord, union; where there is doubt, faith;
> where there is despair, hope; where there is
> darkness, light; where there is sadness, joy.
> Grant that we may not so much seek to
> be consoled as to console; to be understood
> as to understand; to be loved as to love.
> For it is in giving that we receive;
> it is in pardoning that we are pardoned;
> and it is in dying that we are born to
> eternal life. *Amen.*
> *(A prayer attributed to St. Francis)*

And at the Very End

Have the group members assess what they have gained in the session.

- What did you learn?
- Identify any new insights you gained.
- What issues discussed in the session would you like to know more about?

Session 2

Security

Bible Study and Discussion

Begin the session with the Bible reading. The group discussed the concept of peace at the previous meeting. At this session they will explore the personal and communal dimensions of security. The reading is Psalm 20.

Psalm 20

The Lord answer you in the day of trouble!
The name of the God of Jacob protect you!

May he send you help from the sanctuary,
    and give you support from Zion!
May he remember all your offerings,
    and regard with favor your burnt sacrifices!

May he grant you your heart's desire,
    and fulfill all your plans!
May we shout for joy over your victory,
    and in the name of our God set up our banners!
May the Lord fulfill all your petitions!

Now I know that the Lord will help his anointed;
    he will answer him from his holy heaven
    with mighty victories by his right hand.
Some boast of chariots, and some of horses;
    but we boast of the name of the Lord our God.
They will collapse and fall;
    but we shall rise and stand upright.

Talk about Psalm 20. You may want to use these questions to begin the discussion:

1. Historical records show that in 1839 Scottish miners, trapped in a mine near Edinburgh, were heard singing verses 1–4 as they waited for death. Can you identify what there is about these verses that gave the miners strength?

2. "Now I know . . ." is so emphatic in verse 6 that it turns the focus of the Psalm. What is the "knowledge" that allows a person to "boast about the name of Yahweh our God . . . ?"

3. Read and compare Job 10:25–27, Amos 6:1–7 and I Corinthians 13:12.

4. Do you think that the poet of Psalm 20 would agree with Marshal de la Ferte that "God is on the side of the big battalions"?

Moving Along

1. Appendix A contains personal statements from Louis Mountbatten, Omar N. Bradley, Dwight D. Eisenhower, and Jimmy Carter. Read each of these statements (pages 38–47). What message do they give you? What do they have in common?

2. Over two decades separate Presidents Eisenhower and Carter; however, can you identify similar themes in both of their farewell addresses?

3. Eisenhower warns of "misplaced power"; Mountbatten says that nuclear arms have "no military purpose"; Bradley speaks of a "collapse of reason." What legacy are these military leaders bestowing on us?

4. What are the economic questions raised by Guy Halverson, (page 83) and Lloyd Dumas (page 86)?

5. William W. Winpisinger (page 47) speaks from a unique position as a labor leader. What is the "dilemma" he sees for defense workers? Is this equally true for members of minorities?

Discuss:

What is the chance that the Soviets will send their tanks through central Europe? Well, it is a fraction of one percent, but we cannot take a chance on it. And so we devote approximately one-fourth of our defense budget to that fraction of one-percent possibility.

But what is the chance that the Soviets will take advantage of hunger, desperation, and chaos in a developing nation? The chance is 99 percent—and we are talking of cutting back in that area.

—*Representative Paul Simon (D-Ill.)*

Preparing for the Next Session
(Just War)

· The next session addresses the concept of the "just war." The group should be encouraged to reread the Introduction and the articles by Nathaniel Pierce and William Sloane Coffie on pages 55–60 of Appendix A and Edward L. Long, Jr. and John C. Bennett on pages 104–111 of Appendix B.

· Decide on who will be the moderator for the next meeting.

· Since the "just war" and "crusade" are the religious community's response to war, you may want to invite a resource person to make a special presentation.

· Have you considered using audiovisuals?

Ending

· Read aloud: James 4:1–12
· Pause for silent prayer, meditation, and reflection.
· Share prayers and intercessions.
· Read together:

> Almighty God, kindle, we pray, in every heart
> the true love of peace, and guide with your wisdom
> those who take counsel for the nations of the earth;
> that in tranquility your dominion may increase, until
> the earth is filled with the knowledge of your love;
> through Jesus Christ our Lord. *Amen.*

At the Very End

Have the group assess what they have gained from the session.
· What did you learn?
· Identify any new insights you gained.
· What issue discussed in the session would you like to know more about?

Session 3

Just War

Bible Study and Discussion

You have completed two sessions—one focusing on peace, the other on security. This third session reviews and questions the theory of the "just war." The group has been asked to reread the Introduction and the articles in appendices A and B addressing this subject. Begin this session by reading and discussing Colossians 3:12–17.

Colossians 3:12–17

> Put on then, as God's chosen ones, holy and beloved, compassion, kindness, lowliness, meekness, and patience, forbearing one another and, if one has a complaint against another, forgiving each other; as the Lord has forgiven you, so you also must forgive. And above all these put on love, which binds everything together in perfect harmony. And let the peace of Christ rule in your hearts, to which indeed you were called in the one body. And be thankful. Let the word of Christ dwell in you richly, as you teach and admonish one another in all wisdom, and as you sing psalms and hymns and spiritual songs with thankfulness in your hearts to God. And whatever you do, in word or deed, do everything in the name of the Lord Jesus, giving thanks to God the Father through him.

Ask each person to:

• Read this passage of Scripture silently, then have someone read it aloud.

• Discuss the reading, giving special attention to the "virtues" identified: compassion, kindness, lowliness, meekness, patience, and so on.

• How do these Christian attributes compare with the contemporary virtues of courage, determination, aggressiveness, and drive?

• Compare this passage with the one that preceeds it: Colossians 3:5–11.

• How can worship (the author says "psalms and hymns and spiritual songs") bring wisdom and moral perspective?

Moving Along

1. Discuss your understanding of the "just war."

2. How do recent wars fit into the "just war" theory, e.g., World War II, Korea, Vietnam?

3. Who declares that a war or a conflict is "just"? The state? The religious community? The individual?

4. After reviewing the requirements of a "just war," is the theory still operable in the nuclear age?

5. In his article, John Bennett (page 105) poses a serious question: Can war, as we have come to know it, preserve or destroy the future?

6. Is the "just war" theory a cop-out for Christians?

7. What is an immoral country? Do institutions have morals?

Preparing for the Final Session
(Stewardship and Christian Responsibility)

Start planning your last session as a group.

• Is there someone you would like to invite to meet with your group? If there is a seminary or college nearby, you may want to extend an invitation to a member of the faculty to serve as a resource person, e.g., a professor of moral theology or philosophy.

• Do you know how to get in touch with your congressional representative? Does he or she have a local office in your area? Is this person one with whom you'd like to share your discussion?

• Decide on a moderator for the next meeting.

• Suggest that the participants read the articles on pages 67–70 in Appendix A and pages 111–119 in Appendix B before you gather again.

Ending

• Read aloud: Psalm 85:7–13.

• Pause for silent meditation and reflection.

• Share personal prayers and petitions.
• Read aloud:

> *A Memoir*
> With every power for good to stay and guide me,
> comforted and inspired beyond all fear,
> I'll live these days with you in thought beside me,
> and pass, with you, into the coming year,
> Should it be ours to drain the cup of grieving
> even to the dregs of pain, at thy command,
> we will not falter, thankfully receiving all
> that is given by thy loving hand.
> But should it be thy will once more to release
> us to life's enjoyment and its good sunshine,
> that we've learned from sorrow shall increase
> us and all our life be dedicated as thine.
> While all the powers of God aid and attend us,
> boldly we'll face the future, be it what may.
> At even, and at morn, God will befriend us,
> and oh, most surely on each new year's day!
> —*Dietrich Bonhoeffer,*
> *on the eve of his death in 1945*

Read together:

> O God, you have bound us together in a common life. Help us, in
> the midst of our struggles for justice and truth to confront one
> another without hatred or bitterness, and to work together with
> mutual forbearance and respect; through Jesus Christ our Lord.
> *Amen.*

• Suggest that participants in the group write a prayer for the next
session.

And at the Very End
Have the group assess what they have gained from the session.
• What did you learn?
• Identify any new insights you gained.
• What issues discussed in the session would you like to know more
about?

Session 4

Stewardship and Christian Responsibility

Bible Study and Discussion

Begin this final session with the Bible reading. This session addresses the themes of stewardship and Christian responsibility. The Scripture passage recounts the call of the prophet Ezekiel. Someone from the group might like to volunteer to read this selection aloud or the group moderator may choose to do so.

Ezekiel 2:1–7

And he said to me, "Son of man, stand upon your feet, and I will speak with you." And when he spoke to me, the Spirit entered into me and set me upon my feet; and I heard him speaking to me. And he said to me, "Son of man, I send you to the people of Israel, to a nation of rebels, who have rebelled against me; they and their fathers have transgressed against me to this very day. The people also are impudent and stubborn: I send you to them; and you shall say to them, 'Thus says the Lord God.' And whether they hear or refuse to hear (for they are a rebellious house) they will know that there has been a prophet among them. And you, son of man, be not afraid of them, nor be afraid of their words, though briers and thorns are with you and you sit upon scorpions; be not afraid of their words, nor be dismayed at their looks, for they are a rebellious house. And you shall speak my words to them, whether they hear or refuse to hear; for they are a rebellious house.

· Before discussing this passage, you may want to be clear about the role of the Old Testament prophets. Be clear about the difference between prophet, fortune teller, seer, and mystic.

· What does the term "son of man" imply?

· Construct a possible case for Ezekiel's rejection of the call.

· Rewrite this passage to reflect the contemporary world situation.

· Discuss the following quotes from Pope Paul VI:

> "Refusal to undertake this conversion of military-related industries to peace-oriented industries is completely incompatible with the spirit of humanity and still more with the spirit of Christianity" . . . because . . . "it is unthinkable that no other work can be found for hundreds of thousands of workers than the production of instruments of death."

Moving Along

1. Discuss Earl Brill's article (page 22), especially as he urges a return to simple Christian truths in order to understand Christ's teaching about war and violence.

2. William Sloane Coffin quotes Ezekiel's lament over Tyre: "You have corrupted your wisdom for the sake of your splendor." Do you agree that the arms race enhances "status through power"?

3. Bishop Frey asks "What Is Peace?" This is a question the group addressed in Session 1. Have there been any new insights over the past three sessions?

4. Using Glen Stassen's personal testimony as a starting point (page 67), discuss your fears of nuclear war. How does this fear affect you? Does Stassen suggest helpful activities for you and your congregation?

5. Discuss:
The money required to provide adequate food, water, education, health and housing for everyone in the world has been estimated at $17 billion a year. It is a huge sum of money about as much as the world spends on arms every two weeks.

—The New Internationalist

6. Attempt writing a statement that reflects your group's concern. Share this with the whole congregation.

Ending

· Read aloud: Matthew 5:1–16
· Pause for silent prayer, reflection, and meditation.
· Share personal prayers, intercessions, or petitions.
· Read aloud:

He who would valiant be 'Gainst all disaster,
Let him in constancy Follow the Master.
There's no discouragement Shall make him once relent
His first avowed intent To be a pilgrim.

Who so beset him round With dismal stories,
Do but themselves confound, His strength the more is.
No foes shall stay his might, Though he with giants fight;
He will make good his right To be a pilgrim.
Since, Lord, thou dost defend Us with thy Spirit,
We know we at the end Shall life inherit.
Then fancies flee away! I'll fear not what men say,
I'll labor night and day To be a pilgrim.
—*John Bunyan*

• Read together:

Almighty God, kindle, we pray, in every heart the
true love of peace, and guide with your wisdom
those who take counsel for the nations of earth,
that in tranquility your dominion may increase
until the earth is filled with the knowledge
of your love; through Jesus Christ our Lord,
who loves and reigns with you, in the unity of
the Holy Spirit, on God, now and forever.
Amen.

And at the Very End

• Have the group members assess what they have gained in these four sessions.

• Discuss the possibility for continued meetings or joint actions that members of the group can engage in, and circulate a sign-up sheet.

Appendix A:

Personal Testimonies

A CHANGE OF HEART
Earl H. Brill

Where are we, as a nation? What are we up to, and where are we headed? These questions have particular relevance for the religious community, because we believe that God himself is concerned with our national life. To call our country a "nation under God" is not to assert some moral or spiritual superiority, but merely to acknowledge that every nation is under God, that God's will applies to all people, that we are accountable to him for how we use the land, the resources, the freedom, and the opportunities that he has given us.

If we look at ourselves honestly, we see a mixture of good and evil, pluses and minuses. So how we assess our present condition pretty much depends on what we choose to see.

I want to raise some questions about an area of our public life that I view with concern. I'm referring to what appears to be a sudden and hysterical move toward a massive and disastrous arms race that carries with it the threat of economic collapse or even nuclear war. And what concerns me most is that the American people either do not seem to be noticing it, or actually seem to approve of it.

We hear a lot about cuts in the federal budget, reductions in the size and scope of government, tax cuts to stimulate the economy — and even some day balancing the federal budget. Well, the fact is that the overall federal budget is not being reduced at all. The government will spend more next year than this year and even more the following year — *and all that new spending is by the military.* Estimates indicate that it is planned to spend more than a trillion dollars over the next five years. We are committed to buy weapons systems for which the technology does not even exist yet — and never mind the price tag. There is no assurance that any of these expensive toys will do what they are designed for, or that they will serve any useful purpose. We already have more missiles trained on the Soviet Union than we have targets to fire at. We have a nuclear arsenal that is capable of killing everybody in the USSR several times over. And yet we are blithely talking about spending another trillion dollars and nobody seems to mind!

Earl H. Brill is Director of Studies, College of Preachers, Mt. St. Alban, Washington, D.C.

There is nothing partisan about this movement. Politicians of both major parties have jumped in enthusiastically to endorse bigger military budgets. In fact, they are now saying that the spending *itself* is a test of our national will. So the means have become the end. We solve problems by throwing money at them.

It is no mystery why the politicians are unwilling to challenge the new military buildup. Nearly every congressperson has at least one significant defense contractor—and a lot of defense-related jobs — in his or her home district. There is something for everybody. And you don't kill the goose that lays the golden egg. So we have all been bought off. And it is not just politicians. It is everybody. According to recent polls, most of us think we should be spending more on defense, though we do not seem to be clear as to just why.

The usual justification, of course, is that if we do not increase our military arsenal, the Russians "are gonna get us." If we don't spend the extra billion, the Russians are going to land in Washington, or New York, or Kankakee, sooner or later.

Now, there is a certain engaging logic in that position. Nobody — well, almost nobody — would deny that the nation needs an adequate defense. We do have to be prepared for war to keep the peace. But once we grant that point, the big spenders rush right on to the logical conclusion that *any* military expenditure is therefore justifiable, indeed *necessary* to ward off the Russian threat. We have no criteria to distinguish necessary spending from sheer waste — and there is plenty of that.

Every branch of service absolutely needs a whole shopping list of new weapons systems, plus more pay for the troops, plus research and development money for even newer playthings, plus enormous amounts of money to cover the cost overruns of all the other programs. It does add up.

There is a case for adequate defense spending — but the case has not yet been made for this huge new buildup. All we get is a lot of windy rhetoric about how we have to be strong and stand up against the Russians. And that makes us feel tough but it certainly doesn't constitute a rational argument for a new arms race.

We *have* to be realistic — of course the USSR is run by a lot of very tough and mean characters. But the evidence suggests that these people are running scared too. Don't forget that for the past thirty-five years we have had troops stationed all around them, from West Berlin to South Korea. We have flown spy planes and satellites over their territory. We have targeted over 2,000 missiles at their major population centers. And if that's not enough, just remember that they also have to worry about those hundreds of millions of Chinese on their border.

So as we acquire more weapons — the Russians acquire more weapons. We develop a new missile — they develop one. We adopt a more sophisticated technology — they follow suit. After a generation of this escalating arms race, the result has not been national security — it has only been an increase in the level of terror — and we guard ourselves against this simply by not thinking about it. But the terror is there. We now have a nuclear arsenal — let's call things by their right name — atomic and hydrogen bombs — capable of destroying civilization, with no conceivable military objective that any sane human being would use them for. We have been passionately pursuing a security that turns out to be an illusion. And if anybody thinks the next trillion dollars is going to buy security, they are kidding themselves.

This is an issue that goes beyond military policy, beyond economics or foreign affairs, indeed beyond politics. It is a moral and religious issue that calls into question our deepest commitments, our most cherished beliefs, our sense of what it means to be human.

For we share a faith in which peacemakers are perceived as blessed. We worship a God who calls us to turn swords into plowshares and spears into pruning hooks. Jesus reminds us that to love our neighbor is the very essence of God's Law and he himself went beyond that when he commanded us to love even our enemies.

Our religious heritage speaks directly to the illusion of security, the belief that if we just have enough weapons, we will be safe. When Israel put its trust in armies and alliances, Israel collapsed, as the prophets had warned. Jesus himself tells us that he who takes to the sword will perish by the sword. And over and over again, he warned us that whoever would seek to save his life will lose it. This I take to mean that any attempt to ensure a risk-free life is doomed to failure, whether in a person or in a nation.

Our political leaders are following this pointless and dangerous policy because they think they have the people behind them. So if enough of us begin to think through the implications of this new arms race, perhaps that policy can be reversed. After all, the people running the arms race are not vicious merchants of death — they are decent ordinary people like you and me. They are honest and patriotic people doing what they think best. But their self-interest is involved. Their careers, their jobs, their futures, their prestige, their prosperity all serve to lock them into the system, even though the system itself is pointless and destructive. They desperately need to hear from people outside the system who can challenge the basic assumptions of that cozy, self-enclosed world.

What can we do? Well, to start with, we can ask the politicians and the Pentagon for a few simple things.

We can demand that the claims of the military be measured against a coherent strategy for peace: the defense of the nation and the pursuit of our *legitimate* national interests abroad — not the propping up of every regime that calls itself anticommunist. We can demand that our government refrain from trying to solve every international problem by the use of force.

We must return to the strategic arms limitation talks and approve the agreements that have already been reached through the efforts of our last three presidents.

We ought to consider seriously George Kennan's dramatic proposal *(see page 67)* that we and the Russians agree to destroy half of our nuclear weapons, which would still leave both sides with far more than could ever be needed.

We can apply the same financial stringency to the military that is now being applied to all other areas of government — instituting cost controls, demanding cost effectiveness, imposing tough standards and priorities, making do with less.

And we ought to reduce our massive sales of deadly weapons to other countries, so as to reduce the level of armed conflict all over the world.

To move in such a direction would require more than a shift in national policy. It would call for a major change in public opinion — a change of heart, no less. It would call for us to give up, finally, the illusion of security: the fantasy that, in an unsafe world, we can buy safety. It would call for us to give up the illusion of total control, the belief that this country should be able to settle any international or internal dispute anywhere in the world, to our own satisfaction. It calls for massive infusion of courage and hope in a people who have grown accustomed to the pursuit of security, a willingness to take some risks in the name of peace.

Now I realize that these issues are far more complex than I have been able to indicate in these few lines. But you do not have to take my word for any of these things. We appear to be in the opening stages of a great national debate on defense policy, military spending, and global strategy.

As responsible Christians and citizens, we must get into that debate, to inform ourselves on the subject, for it may be the most important issue to face us as a nation. It may decide our future and our children's future — and we all have a very high stake in the outcome.

If we are to move our national defense policy into a new and peaceful direction, that movement will have to begin in the churches, with the people who serve a Lord who tells us that if we seek to save our life we will lose it; a Lord who willingly gave up his own life rather than reaching for a sword. That Lord promised us neither safety nor security, but did promise to be with us and to support us as we seek to do his will. And his will for us is peace. Surely a policy of restraint and moderation in the humble pursuit of peace is in the best American tradition — and is the only policy worthy of a great nation.

THE ONLY WAY OUT OF THE NUCLEAR NIGHTMARE IS BY A BOLD AND SWEEPING GESTURE
George Kennan

What can we do?

Adequate words are lacking to express the full seriousness of our present situation. It is not just that the United States is for the moment on a collision course politically with the Soviet Union, and that the process of rational communication between the two governments seems to have broken down completely; it is also — and even more importantly — the fact that the ultimate

George Kennan is professor emeritus at the Institute for Advanced Study, Princeton University, and a former U.S. ambassador to the Soviet Union (1952–53) and Yugoslavia (1961–63).

sanction behind the conflicting policies of these two governments is a type and volume of weaponry which could not possibly be used without utter disaster for us all.

For over thirty years wise and far-seeing people have been warning us about the futility of any war fought with nuclear weapons and about the dangers involved in their cultivation. Some of the first of these voices to be raised were those of great scientists including outstandingly that of Albert Einstein himself. But there has been no lack of others. Every president of this country, from Dwight Eisenhower to Jimmy Carter, has tried to remind us that there could be no such thing as victory in a war fought with such weapons. So have a great many other eminent persons.

When one looks back today over the history of these warnings, one has the impression that something has been lost of the sense of urgency, the hopes, and the excitement that initially inspired them so many years ago. One senses, even on the part of those who today most acutely perceive the problem and are inwardly most exercised about it, a certain discouragement, resignation, perhaps even despair, when it comes to the question of raising the subject again.

The danger is so obvious. So much has already been said. What is to be gained by reiteration? What good would it now do? Look at the record. Over all these years the competition in the development of nuclear weaponry has proceeded steadily, relentlessly, without the faintest regard for all these warning voices. We have gone on piling weapon upon weapon, missile upon missile, new levels of destructiveness upon old ones. We have done this helplessly, almost involuntarily — like the victims of some sort of hypnotism, like men in a dream, like lemmings heading for the sea, like the children of Hamlin marching blindly along behind their Pied Piper.

And the result is that we have achieved, we and the Russians together, in the creation of these devices and their means of delivery, levels of redundancy of such grotesque dimensions as to defy rational understanding.

I say redundancy. I know of no better way to describe it. But actually, the word redundancy is too mild. It implies that there could be levels of these weapons that would not be redundant. Personally, I doubt that there could. I question whether these devices are really weapons at all. A true weapon is at best something with which you endeavor to affect the behavior of another society by influencing the minds, the calculations, the intentions, of the men that control it; it is not something with which you destroy indiscriminately the lives, the substance, the hopes, the culture, the civilization, of another people. What a confession of intellectual poverty it would be — what a bankruptcy of intelligent statesmanship — if we had to admit that such blind, senseless acts of destruction were the best use we could make of what we have come to view as the leading elements of our military strength!

To my mind, the nuclear bomb is the most useless weapon ever invented. It can be employed to no rational purpose. It is not even an effective defense against itself. It is only something with which, in a moment of petulance or panic, you commit such fearful acts of destruction as no sane person would ever wish to have upon his conscience.

There are those who will agree, with a sigh, to much of what I have just said, but will point to the need for something called deterrence. This is, of course, a concept which attributes to others — to others who, like ourselves, were born of women, walk on two legs, and love their children — to human beings, in short, the most fiendish and inhuman of tendencies. But all right: accepting for the sake of argument the profound iniquity of these adversaries, no one could deny, I think, that the present Soviet and American arsenals, presenting over a million times the destructive power of the Hiroshima bomb, are simply fantastically redundant to the purpose in question.

If the same relative proportions were to be preserved, something well less than twenty percent of these stocks would surely suffice for the most sanguine concepts of deterrence, whether as between the two nuclear superpowers or with relation to any of those other governments that have been so ill-advised as to enter upon the nuclear path. Whatever their suspicions of each other, there can be no excuse on the part of these two governments for holding, poised against each other and poised in a sense against the whole northern hemisphere, quantities of these weapons so vastly in excess of any rational and demonstrable requirements.

How have we got ourselves into this dangerous mess? Let us not confuse the question by blaming it all on our Soviet adversaries. They have, of course, their share of the blame, and not least in their cavalier dismissal of the Baruch Plan so many years ago. They too have made their mistakes, and I should be the last to deny it. But we must remember that it has been we Americans who, at almost every step of the road, have taken the lead in the development of this sort of weaponry. It was we who first produced and tested such a device; we who were the first to raise its destructiveness to a new level with the hydrogen bomb; we who introduced the multiple warhead; we who have declined every proposal for the renunciation of the principle of "first use"; and we alone, so help us God, who have used the weapon in anger against others, and against tens of thousands of helpless noncombatants at that.

I know that reasons were offered for some of these things. I know that others might have taken this sort of a lead had we not done so. But let us not, in the face of this record, so lose ourselves in self-righteousness and hypocrisy as to forget our own measure of complicity in creating the situation we face today.

What is it then, if not our own will, and if not the supposed wickedness of our components, that has brought us to this pass?

The answer, I think, is clear. It is primarily the inner momentum, the independent momentum, of the weapons race itself — the compulsions that arise and take charge of great powers when they enter upon a competition with each other in the building up of major armaments of any sort.

Is it possible to break out of this charmed and vicious circle? It is sobering to recognize that no one, at least to my knowledge, has yet done so. But no one, for that matter, has ever been faced with such great catastrophe, such unalterable catastrophe, at the end of the line. Others, in earlier decades, could befuddle themselves with dreams of something called "victory." We, perhaps fortunately, are denied this seductive prospect. We have to break out of the circle. We have no other choice.

How are we to do it?

I must confess that I see no possibility of doing this by means of discussions along the lines of the negotiations that have been in progress, off and on, over this past decade, under the acronym of SALT. I regret, to be sure, that the most recent SALT agreement has not been ratified. I regret it, because if the benefits to be expected from that agreement were slight, its disadvantages were even slighter; and it had a symbolic value which should not have been so lightly sacrificed.

But I have, I repeat, no illusion that negotiations on the SALT pattern — negotiations, that is, in which each side is obsessed with the chimera of relative advantage and strives only to retain a maximum of the weaponry for itself while putting its opponent to the maximum disadvantage — I have no illusion that such negotiations could ever be adequate to get us out of this hole. They are not a way of escape from the weapons race, they are an integral part of it.

Whoever does not understand that when it comes to nuclear weapons, the whole concept of relative advantage is illusory — whoever does not understand that when you are talking about absurd and preposterous quantities of overkill the relative sizes of arsenals have no serious meaning — whoever does not understand that the danger lies not in the possibility that someone else might have more missiles and warheads than we do but in the very existence of these unconscionable quantities of highly poisonous explosives, and their existence, above all, in hands as weak and shaky and undependable as those of ourselves or our adversaries or any other mere human beings. Whoever does not understand these things is never going to guide us out of this increasingly dark and menacing forest of bewilderments into which we have all wandered.

I can see no way out of this dilemma other than by a bold and sweeping departure — a departure that would cut surgically through the exaggerated anxieties, the self-engendered nightmares, and the sophisticated mathematics of destruction, in which we have all been entangled over these recent years, and would permit us to move, with courage and decision, to the heart of the problem.

President Reagan recently said, and I think very wisely, that he would "negotiate as long as necessary to reduce the numbers of nuclear weapons to a point where neither side threatens the survival of the other." Now that is, of course, precisely the thought to which these present observations of mine are addressed. But I wonder whether the negotiations would really have to be at such great length?

What I would like to see the President do, after due consultation with the Congress, would be to propose to the Soviet government an immediate across-the-boards reduction by fifty percent of the nuclear arsenals now being maintained by the two superpowers — a reduction affecting in equal measure all forms of the weapon — strategic, medium range, and tactical — as well as all means of their delivery — all this to be implemented at once and without further wrangling among the experts, and to be subject to such national means of verification as now lie at the disposal of the two powers.

Whether the balance of reduction would be precisely even — whether it could be construed to favor statistically one side or the other — would not be the question. Once we start thinking that way, we would be back on the same old fateful track that has brought us where we are today. Whatever the precise results of such a reduction, there would still be plenty of overkill left — so much so that if this first operation were successful, I would then like to see a second one put in hand to rid us of at least two-thirds of what would be left.

Now I have, of course, no idea of the scientific aspects of such an operation; but I can imagine that serious problems might be presented by the task of removing, and disposing safely of, the radioactive contents of the many thousands of warheads that would have to be dismantled. Should this be the case, I would like to see the President couple his appeal for a fifty percent reduction with the proposal that there be established a joint Soviet-American scientific committee, under the chairmanship of a distinguished neutral figure, to study jointly and in all humility the problem not only of the safe disposal of these wastes but also the question of how they could be utilized in such a way as to make a positive contribution to human life, either in the two countries themselves or — perhaps preferably — elsewhere. In such a joint scientific venture we might both atone for some of our past follies and lay the foundation for a more constructive relationship.

It will be said: This proposal, whatever its merits, deals with only a part of the problem. This is perfectly true. Behind it there would still lurk the serious political differences that now divide us from the Soviet government. Behind it would still lie the problems recently treated, and still to be treated, in the SALT forum. Behind it would still lie the great question of the acceptability of war itself, any war, even a conventional one, as a means of solving problems among great industrial powers in this age of high technology.

What has been suggested here would not prejudice the continued treatment of these questions just as today, in whatever forums and under whatever safeguards the two powers find necessary. The conflicts and arguments over these questions could all still proceed to the heart's content of all those who view them with such passionate commitment. The stakes would simply be smaller; and that would be a great relief to all of us.

What I have suggested is, of course, only a beginning. But a beginning has to be made somewhere; and if it has to be made, it is best that it should be made where the dangers are the greatest, and their necessity the least. If a step of this nature could be successfully taken, people might find the heart to tackle with greater confidence and determination the many problems that would still remain.

It will be argued that there would be risks involved. Possibly so. I do not see them. I do not deny the possibility. But if there are, so what? Is it possible to conceive of any dangers greater than those that lie at the end of the collision course on which we are now embarked? And if not, why choose the greater — why choose, in fact, the greatest — of all risks, in the hopes of avoiding the lesser ones?

We are confronted here with two courses. At the end of the one lies hope — faint hope, if you will — uncertain hope, hope surrounded with dangers, if you insist. At the end of the other lies, so far as I am able to see, no hope at all. Can there be — in the light of our duty not just to ourselves (for we are all going to die sooner or later) but of our duty to our own kind, our duty to the continuity of the generations, our duty to the great experiment of civilized life on this rare and rich and marvelous planet — can there be, in the light of these claims on our loyalty, any question as to which course we should adopt?

In the final week of his life, Albert Einstein signed the last of the collective appeals against the development of nuclear weapons that he was ever to sign. He was dead before it appeared. It was an appeal drafted, I gather, by Bertrand Russell. I had my differences with Russell at the time, as I do now in retrospect; but I would like to quote one sentence from the final paragraph of the statement, not only because it was the last one Einstein ever signed, but because it sums up, I think, all that I have to say on the subject. It reads as follows:

"We appeal, as human beings to human beings: Remember your humanity, and forget the rest."

NUCLEAR WAR: "A FRANKENSTEIN"
Douglas MacArthur

The last time I spoke before this august body, the war still raged outside. The crash of guns rattled windows, the sputter of musketry drowned voices, the acrid smell of smoke filled our nostrils, the stench of death was everywhere. And now, sixteen years later, although those incidents have become but dark memory, the possibility of war still hangs like a cloud before our eyes. It overshadows all other problems, intruding upon every thought and action, encompassing all that we hold most dear, dictating not only the present but our very future.

Many in this brilliant audience were my former comrades in arms. They have known war in all its horror and, as veterans, hope against its recurrence. How, they well may ask, did such an institution as war become so integrated with man's life and civilization? How has it grown to be the most vital factor in our existence?

It started in a modest enough way as a sort of gladiatorial method of settling disputes between conflicting tribes. One of the oldest and most classical examples is the biblical story of David and Goliath. Each of the two contesting groups selected its champion. They fought and, based upon the outcome, an agreement resulted. Then, as time went on, small professional groups known as armies fought in some obscure corner of the globe, and victory or defeat was accepted as the basis of an enduring peace.

And from then on, down through the ages, the constant record is an increase in the character and strength of the forces, with the rate of increase always accelerating. From a small percentage of the population it finally engulfed all. It is now the nation in arms.

General MacArthur delivered this speech before a joint session of the Congress of the Philippines on 5 July 1961.

Within the span of my own life, I have witnessed much of this evolution. At the turn of the century, when I joined the Army, the target was one enemy casualty at the end of a rifle, a pistol, a bayonet, a sword. Then came the machine gun, designed to kill by the dozen. After that, the heavy artillery — raining death upon the hundreds. Then the aerial bomb to strike by the thousands — followed by the atom explosion to reach the hundreds of thousands.

Now, electronics and other processes of science have raised the destructive potential to encompass millions. And with restless hands we work feverishly in dark laboratories to find the means to destroy all at one blow.

But this very triumph of scientific annihilation — this very success of invention — has destroyed the possibility of war's being a medium for the practical settlement of international differences. The enormous destruction to both sides of closely matched opponents makes it impossible for even the winner to translate it into anything but his own disaster.

The last war, even with its now antiquated armaments, clearly demonstrated that the victor had to bear in large part the very injuries inflicted on his foe. My own country expended billions of dollars and untold energies to heal the wounds of Germany and Japan.

Global war has become a Frankenstein to destroy both sides. No longer is it a weapon of adventure — the shortcut to international power. If you lose, you are annihilated. If you win, you stand only to lose. No longer does it possess even the chance of the winner of a duel. It contains now only the germs of double suicide.

Time was when victory in war represented economic wealth, accelerated prosperity, a place in the international sun. It was the final weapon of statecraft, the apotheosis of political diplomacy. Its application, however, was regulated, controlled, and limited by the basic principle that a great nation that enters upon war and does not see it through to victory must ultimately suffer all the consequences of defeat. That is what happened to us in Korea. With victory within our grasp, and without the use of the atom bomb which we needed no more then than against Japan, we failed to see it through.

Had we done so, we would have destroyed Red China's capability of waging modern war for generations to come. Our failure to win that war was a major disaster for the free world. Its fatal consequences are now increasingly being felt in the military rise of Red China into a mighty colossus which threatens all of Asia and bids fair to emerge as the balance of military power in the world. This would jeopardize freedom on all continents.

But the conditions that prevailed in the Korean War exist no longer and will come no more. Then we were the sole possessor of nuclear power. We stood alone in military might. Now all is changed. Others possess this weapon. Relative strengths from now on will probably change little with the years. Action by one will promptly be matched by reaction from the other.

The great question is: Can global war now be outlawed from the world? If so, it would mark the greatest advance in civilization since the Sermon on the Mount. It would lift at one stroke the darkest shadow which has engulfed mankind from the beginning. It would not only remove fear and bring security

— it would not only create new moral and spiritual values — it would produce an economic wave of prosperity that would raise the world's standard of living beyond anything ever dreamed of by man.

The hundreds of billions of dollars now spent in mutual preparedness could conceivably abolish poverty from the face of the earth. It would accomplish even more than this; it would at one stroke reduce the international tensions that seem to be insurmountable now to matters of more probable solution. This would not, of course, mean the abandonment of all armed forces, but it would reduce them to the simpler problems of internal order and international police. It would not mean utopia at one fell stroke, but it would mean that the great roadblock now existing to the development of the human race would have been cleared.

You will say at once that, although the abolition of war has been the dream of man for centuries, every proposition to that end has been promptly discarded as impossible and fantastic. But that was before the science of the past decade made mass destruction a reality. The argument then was along spiritual and moral lines, and lost. But now the tremendous evolution of nuclear and other potentials of destruction has suddenly taken the problem away from its primary consideration as a moral and spiritual question and brought it abreast of scientific realism. It is no longer an ethical equation to be pondered solely by learned philosophers and ecclesiastics, but a hard-core one for the decision of the masses whose survival is the issue.

This is as true of the Soviet side of the world as of the free side — as true behind the Iron Curtain as in front of it. The ordinary people of the world, whether free or slave, are all in agreement on this solution; and this perhaps is the only thing in the world they do agree upon, but it is the most vital and determinate of all. We are told we must go on indefinitely as at present — with what at the end, none says — there is no definite objective. They but pass along to those that follow the search for a final solution. And at the end, the problem will be exactly that which we face now.

It may take another cataclysm of destruction to prove the bald truth that the further evolution of civilization cannot take place until global war is abolished. But this is the one issue upon which both sides can agree, for it is the one issue upon which both sides will profit equally. It is the one issue in which the interests of both are completely parallel. It is the one issue which, if settled, may well settle all others.

The present tensions with their threat of national annihilation are fostered by two great illusions. The one, a complete belief on the part of the Soviet world that the capitalistic countries are preparing to attack them; that sooner or later we intend to strike. And the other, a complete belief on the part of the capitalistic countries that the Soviets are preparing to attack us; that sooner or later they intend to strike.

Both are wrong. Each side, so far as the masses are concerned, is desirous of peace. Both dread war. But the constant acceleration of preparation may, without specific intent, ultimately precipitate a kind of spontaneous combustion.

Many will tell you with mockery and ridicule that the abolition of war can be only a dream — that it is but the vague imagining of a visionary. But we must go on or we will go under. And the great criticism that can be made is that the world lacks a plan that will enable us to go on.

We are in a new era. The old methods and solutions no longer suffice. We must have new thoughts, new ideas, new concepts. We must break out of the straitjacket of the past. We must have sufficient imagination and courage to translate the universal wish for peace — which is rapidly becoming a universal necessity — into actuality. And, until then, at whatever cost or sacrifice, we must be fully prepared — lest we perish.

THE RACE TO NUCLEAR WAR
Gene R. LaRocque

In appraising where we stand today, it is difficult to avoid a paralyzing pessimism. We seem to be in the grip of malevolent forces over which we have no control. Individual human beings plead for peace, a reduction in tensions, and a lifting of the burden of armaments. But governments have not been responsive. On the contrary, tensions have increased as action and reaction spur nations to acquire nuclear and conventional weapons at a faster and faster rate. My government and many others ignore the urgent appeals of those millions in the world who seek to avoid nuclear war.

The series of Strategic Arms Limitation Agreements [SALT] between the United States and the Soviet Union, and the modest improvement of relations between the United States and the Soviet Union in the early 1970s, created hopes that armaments could be controlled. But these hopes were crushed by Afghanistan and the rush by the United States to acquire new weapons. Can it be that governments are not aware of the ardent desire by people everywhere for peaceful solutions to inter-nation differences?

It is increasingly clear that nuclear war is an unrelenting and growing threat to hundreds of millions of people. World War III with nuclear weapons *can* happen and almost certainly *will* happen unless all governments confront this most uncomfortable reality.

Each new weapon introduced, each new resort to military force, increases the likelihood of nuclear war. You and I and our children have a good chance of being destroyed by nuclear weapons before the year 2000, unless positive steps are taken to avoid this catastrophe.

The United States and the Soviet Union are in the grip of insecurity and fear. Both countries offer themselves as leaders but their objectives appear in conflict

Rear Admiral (ret.) Gene La Rocque is the director of the Center for Defense Information, Washington, D.C. His remarks are taken from a speech before the United Nations 19 June 1980.

and in competition, not in the constructive bridging of differences or the recognition of common interests. Recent force reduction proposals by the Soviet Union have been rejected by the U.S. government as propaganda. The United States appears to have declared a moratorium on arms control initiatives. But neither words nor silence will limit arms. Actions by either the United States or the Soviet Union are required to slow the spiraling arms race.

To date there is little evidence that either the United States or the Soviet Union has any desire to curtail nuclear weapons. In January 1970 the United States had 4,000 strategic nuclear weapons to launch against the Soviet Union and China. By any reasonable military standard, this was more than enough to ensure the deaths of millions and the destruction of China and the Soviet Union. Today, the United States has 10,000 thermonuclear weapons available for a prompt and sustained attack on the Soviet Union. In the next ten years, the United States plans to continue this race to nuclear war. By involving its allies in Europe, the United States will have the capability to cause 19,000 nuclear explosions in the Soviet Union by the year 1990. This continuing vast increase in the number of nuclear explosions that U.S. planners feel is necessary defies rational explanation.

Clearly, there is no basis for the myth of the military weakness or passivity of the United States. It must be bluntly stated. The United States has led the nuclear arms race from the beginning, and all indications are it will continue to do so in the future. The United States leads in developing and producing new delivery systems and in the numbers of nuclear weapons for every aspect of warfare. This era of U.S. world leadership may be remembered — by those who survive — as the beginning of the end.

The determination of the United States to increase its military effectiveness it not limited to nuclear weapons. Although, as U.S. Secretary of Defense Harold Brown stated, by most relevant measures the United States remains the military equal or superior to the Soviet Union, the United States is embarked on a vast expansion of its war-fighting capability. Together with its military allies in Europe and Japan, the United States is preparing for nuclear and conventional war on a major scale. Without exception, the United States is urging all its allies in Europe and Japan to increase preparations for war through the acquisition of more destructive weapons and the expenditure of large sums of money. Following the lead of the United States, Western Europe and Japan appear to have abandoned arms limitations in favor of the arms increases.

Either in response to United States actions, or at its own volition, the Soviet Union appears to be doing everything it can to keep up with the United States in developing, testing, and deploying nuclear weapons. In 1970 the Soviet Union was lagging far behind with 1,800 nuclear weapons. Today after a vigorous, expensive effort, the Soviets — with 6,000 nuclear weapons aimed at the United States and China — are still well behind the United States. By a gigantic effort in the next ten years, the Soviet Union could possibly match the United States and acquire enough weapons to cause 19,000 nuclear explosions in the United States. Great Britain, France, and China will also increase nuclear arsenals in the next ten years. We might well refer to the next ten years as the decade of destruction. . . .

Although many American military men talk confidently about their ability to fight and win wars with nuclear weapons, their views are not universally shared. Lord Mountbatten, perhaps *the* leading military officer of the twentieth century, was one of those who argued against the use of nuclear weapons shortly before his tragic death. (See page 38)

My own experience as a career naval officer of the United States led me to a similar conclusion. If nuclear weapons are used in the next war — and there will be more wars — the devastation and deaths will destroy civilization in the northern half of our planet and bring hunger and disease to Asia, Africa, and Latin America. If we continue on the course we are headed, the next war will be a nuclear war and very likely the last one humans will ever fight. It will be the ultimate irony if our own technological genius is the cause of our own destruction. According to estimates of the United States National Security Council, 140 million Americans and 113 million Russians would at once perish.

The illusion that nuclear war could be controlled and limited and used to achieve some practical objective is fed by intoxicating technological developments. Refinements of superaccurate missiles, computers, and satellites lead many technicians and bureaucrats to think in terms of a controlled nuclear war. The illusion of "controlled nuclear war" has been spawned by war games and the persistent assumption that in every war there is a winner. There will be no winners in a nuclear war. But the growing acceptance of the idea that nuclear war can be fought and won increases the likelihood that people everywhere will be the losers.

Nuclear war remains an abstract and unreal concept for most individuals. In the United States most people believe nuclear war would not result in total destruction. Americans feel it may be necessary to risk war to maintain world peace, and many Americans accept the inevitability of a third world war. To most Americans, winning the next war has become more important than avoiding it. They do not comprehend that nuclear war will be entirely different from past wars which have for generations been won and lost in Europe, Asia, and Latin America. Nuclear war is not a means by which the forces of good vanquish the forces of evil. In a nuclear war, both good and evil will perish.

Perhaps the governments of the world will do little to prevent nuclear war until one of these weapons explodes or a major nuclear accident occurs. Perhaps if the United States and the Soviet Union again go to the brink of war as they did in 1962 over Cuba, the sobering effect of such an experience could prompt a more serious attempt to avoid war. But both of these potentially catalytic events have the singular defect that they could easily escalate into the very worldwide disaster we want to prevent.

Three incidents over the past year have dramatized the dangers we face: The natural disaster of the eruption of Mount St. Helens, the near-nuclear disaster at Three Mile Island, and the computer errors which brought us close to nuclear war.

The eruption of Mount St. Helens, while unrelated to nuclear war, gave

Americans a vivid example of an explosion the size of a single, multimegaton, nuclear bomb. Its roar was heard two hundred miles away, and in less than seven days a cloud of volcanic gas and ash containing toxic chemicals spread across our land. Only a few nuclear explosions with radioactive clouds would spread destruction and death across all of North America.

Of the Three Mile Island nuclear plant accident, President Carter put it best when he said:

> I hope that one result of that fright will be to remind every American how vastly more destructive to a hundred million American people, almost half our population, a nuclear exchange would be . . . between us and the Soviet Union. It is the most serious threat we face.

I wish sincerely the actions of our government would reflect the declarations of our President.

This month, computer errors reminded us how dangerously close we are to nuclear catastrophe. A computer erroneously indicated that Soviet submarine-launched rockets would land in the United States within fifteen minutes. U.S. bombers and missiles were readied for immediate launching.

The error was discovered in three minutes, and in twenty minutes the alert was canceled. In the past year three false warnings activated U.S. nuclear forces.

In a statement incident to signing an agreement with the Russians on reducing the risk of the accidental outbreak of nuclear war, the U.S. government warned:

> Despite the most elaborate precautions, it is conceivable that technical malfunction or human failure, a misinterpreted incident or unauthorized action, could trigger a nuclear disaster or nuclear war.

The near collapse of the U.S.-Soviet relations has increased the likelihood of nuclear war and it is clear many governments of the world have chosen to increase preparations for war at a time in history when the emphasis should be against war.

As an American, I am particularly disturbed by the bellicose mood of the people of the United States. The burden of our military actions in Southeast Asia and events in Afghanistan have engendered a feeling of frustration which is dangerous for us and for the rest of the world.

These trends are isolating the United States from its traditional friends. Our allies in Europe, Asia, and Latin America worry more and more about the apparent increase in emphasis the United States is placing on the use of military force to accomplish its objectives in foreign countries. Western Europeans in particular are increasingly apprehensive about the direction and quality of American leadership. They evidence little enthusiasm to follow the United States into a new cold war and a remilitarized foreign policy. Europe's leaders consistently indicate their desire to follow the leadership of the United States only if that leadership moves toward peaceful solutions and a reduction of military stockpiles. Detente may survive elsewhere but in the United States the demise of detente appears welcome.

There is a growing awareness among Europeans that Americans are planning, equipping, and training to fight a limited nuclear war in Europe. There is growing evidence of opposition among both peoples and governments in Europe to this development. In the past, the direction of leadership in the Atlantic Alliance generally flowed from the United States to Europe but, on the pressing issues of war and peace today, leadership may have to flow from Europe to America. Europeans may be able to help persuade their American friends that a belligerent attitude will not preserve the peace. . . .

The activities of individuals and groups often seem small and inadequate in the face of the magnitude of problems, the strength of the opposition, or the indifference of millions. But there is a realistic hope that you and I can help turn things around. American public opinion is notoriously transitory and shifts quickly on foreign policy. There is a cyclical pattern of aggressive and peaceful orientations. While we are in an aggressive phase now, it could become more receptive to reason.

While the United States is hostile to the Soviet Union, an almost cyclical pattern of hostility followed by detente has characterized U.S. relations as well. There are powerful forces that should drive rational leaders to seek mutual accommodation and understanding. We all live on the same small, fragile planet, and sustained hostility endangers the planet. The alternatives of mutual survival or mutual suicide are stark.

Representatives of nongovernmental organizations and research institutes can hasten the return to reason and mutual accommodation through educational activities and pressure on all governments of the world. I would place four items at the top of the list of the immediate agenda that all nations should press on the United States and the Soviet Union. These steps must be achieved quickly and without delay. These are, first, immediate ratification of the SALT II Treaty. Second, a total ban on all nuclear weapons tests. Third, the removal of all nuclear weapons from central Europe or at least a moratorium on the introduction of new nuclear weapons for Europe. And fourth, a declaration by both the United States and the Soviet Union that they will never be the first to use nuclear weapons. There are other important steps which can and should be taken, but these four are the ones I believe to be most important in the short term if we are to avoid a nuclear war.

We and our governments can make a new beginning in the 1980s. The practical necessity of preventing nuclear war is no longer a matter of romantic idealism or wishful thinking. Prevention of nuclear war is the most pragmatic policy for our times. We who point to the danger of nuclear war are the realists. Those who deny this danger, live in a dream world.

Without these prompt actions, we face a decade of destruction. Permit me to conclude with a quote from a distinguished American military man, General Eisenhower, shortly before he died:

But above all, the people, I'd like to believe that the people in the long run are going to do more to promote peace than our governments. Indeed, I think that people want peace so much that one of these days governments better get out of their way and let them have it.

ON THE BRINK OF THE FINAL ABYSS
Earl Louis Mountbatten

Do the frightening facts about the arms race, which show that we are rushing headlong toward a precipice, make any of those responsible for this disastrous course pull themselves together and reach for the brakes?

The answer is "no" and I only wish that I could be the bearer of the glad tidings that there has been a change of attitude and we are beginning to see a steady rate of disarmament. Alas, that is not the case.

I am deeply saddened when I reflect on how little has been achieved in spite of all the talk there has been particularly about nuclear disarmament. There have been numerous international conferences and negotiations on the subject and we have all nursed dreams of a world at peace but to no avail. Since the end of the Second World War, thirty-four years ago, we have had war after war. There is still armed conflict going on in several parts of the world. We live in an age of extreme peril because every war today carries the danger that it could spread and involve the superpowers.

And here lies the greatest danger of all. A military confrontation between the nuclear powers could entail the horrifying risk of nuclear warfare. The Western powers and the USSR started by producing and stockpiling nuclear weapons as a deterrent to general war. The idea seemed simple enough. Because of the enormous amount of destruction that could be wreaked by a single nuclear explosion, the idea was that both sides in what we still see as an East-West conflict would be deterred from taking any aggressive action which might endanger the vital interests of the other.

It was not long, however, before smaller nuclear weapons of various designs were produced and deployed for use in what was assumed to be a tactical or theatre war. The belief was, that were hostilities ever to break out in Western Europe, such weapons could be used in field warfare without triggering an all-out nuclear exchange leading to the final holocaust.

I have never found this idea credible. I have never been able to accept the reasons for the belief that any class of nuclear weapons can be categorized in terms of their tactical or strategic purposes.

Earl Louis Mountbatten was the last Viceroy of India and First Sea Lord of the British Navy. He was killed by a terrorist bomb in Ireland in 1979.

Next month I enter my eightieth year. I am one of the few survivors of the First World War who rose to high command in the Second and I know how impossible it is to pursue military operations in accordance with fixed plans and agreements. In warfare the unexpected is the rule and no one can anticipate what an opponent's reaction will be to the unexpected.

As a sailor I saw enough death and destruction at sea but I also had the opportunity of seeing the absolute destruction of the war zone of the western front in the First World War, where those who fought in the trenches had an average expectation of life of only a few weeks.

Then in 1943 I became Supreme Allied Commander in South-East Asia and saw death and destruction on an even greater scale. But that was all conventional warfare and, horrible as it was, we all felt we had a "fighting" chance of survival. In the event of a nuclear war there will be no chances, there will be no survivors — all will be obliterated.

I am not asserting this without having deeply thought about the matter. When I was chief of the British Defense Staff I made my views known. I have heard the arguments against this view but I have never found them convincing. So I repeat, in all sincerity as a military man I can see no use for any nuclear weapons which would not end in escalation, with consequences that no one can conceive.

And nuclear devastation is not science fiction — it is a matter of fact. Thirty-four years ago there was the terrifying experience of the two atomic bombs that effaced the cities of Hiroshima and Nagasaki off the map. In describing the nightmare a Japanese journalist wrote as follows:

> Suddenly a glaring whitish, pinkish light appeared in the sky accompanied by an unnatural tremor which was followed almost immediately by a wave of suffocating heat and a wind which swept away everything in its path. Within a few seconds the thousands of people in the streets in the centre of the town were scorched by a wave of searing heat. Many were killed instantly, others lay writhing on the ground screaming in agony from the intolerable pain of their burns. Everything standing upright in the way of the blast — walls, houses, factories and other buildings, was annihilated . . . Hiroshima had ceased to exist.

But that is not the end of the story. We remember the tens and tens of thousands who were killed instantly or — worse still — those who suffered a slow painful death from the effect of the burns — we forget that many are still dying horribly from the delayed effects of radiation. To this knowledge must be added the fact that we now have missiles a thousand times as dreadful; I repeat, a thousand times as terrible.

One or two nuclear strikes on this great city of Strasbourg with what today would be regarded as relatively low-yield weapons would utterly destroy all that we see around us and immediately kill probably half its population. Imagine what the picture would be if larger nuclear strikes were to be leveled against not just Strasbourg but ten other cities in, say, a two hundred-mile radius. Or even worse, imagine what the picture would be if there was an unrestrained exchange of nuclear weapons — and this is the most appalling risk of all since, as I have already said, I cannot imagine a situation in which nuclear weapons would be used as battlefield weapons without the conflagration spreading.

Could we not take steps to make sure that these things never come about? A new world war can hardly fail to involve the all-out use of nuclear weapons. Such a war would not drag on for years. It could all be over in a matter of days.

And when it is all over what will the world be like? Our fine great buildings, our homes will exist no more. The thousands of years it took to develop our civilization will have been in vain. Our works of art will be lost. Radio, television, newspapers will disappear. There will be no means of transport. There will be no hospitals. No help can be expected for the few mutilated survivors in any town to be sent from a neighboring town — there will be no neighboring towns left, no neighbors, there will be no help, there will be no hope.

How can we stand by and do nothing to prevent the destruction of our world? Einstein, whose centenary we celebrate this year, was asked to prophesy what weapons would be used in a third world war. I am told he replied to the following effect:

"On the assumption that a third world war must escalate to nuclear destruction, I can tell you what the fourth world war will be fought with — bows and arrows."

The facts about the global nuclear arms race are well known and, as I have already said, SIPRI [Stockholm International Peace Research Institute] has played its part in disseminating authoritative material on world armaments and the need for international efforts to reduce them. But how do we set about achieving practical measures of nuclear arms control and disarmament?

To begin with, we are most likely to preserve the peace if there is a military balance of strength between East and West. The real need is for both sides to replace the attempts to maintain a balance through ever increasing and ever more costly nuclear armaments by a balance based on mutual restraint. Better still, by reduction of nuclear armaments I believe it should be possible to achieve greater security at a lower level of military confrontation.

I regret enormously the delays which the Americans and Russians have experienced in reaching a SALT II agreement for the limitation of even one major class of nuclear weapons with which it deals. I regret even more the fact that opposition to reaching any agreement, which would bring about a restraint in the production and deployment of nuclear weapons, is becoming so powerful in the United States. What can their motives be?

As a military man who has given half a century of active service I say in all sincerity that the nuclear arms race has no military purpose. Wars cannot be fought with nuclear weapons. Their existence only adds to our perils because of the illusions which they have generated.

There are powerful voices around the world who still give credence to the old Roman precept — if you desire peace, prepare for war. This is absolute nuclear nonsense and I repeat — it is a disastrous misconception to believe that by increasing the total uncertainty one increases one's own certainty.

This year we have already seen the beginnings of a miracle. Through the courageous determination of Presidents Carter and Sadat and Prime Minister Begin we have seen the first real move toward what we all hope will be a lasting peace between Egypt and Israel. Their journey has only just begun and the path they have chosen will be long and fraught with disappointments and obstacles. But these bold leaders have realized the alternatives and have faced up to their duty in a way which those of us who hunger for the peace of the world applaud.

Is it possible that this initiative will lead to the start of yet another even more vital miracle and someone somewhere will take that first step along the long stony road which will lead to an effective form of nuclear arms limitation, including the banning of tactical nuclear weapons?

After all, it is true that science offers us almost unlimited opportunities, but it is up to us, the people, to make the moral and philosophical choices and since the threat to humanity is the work of human beings, it is up to man to save himself from himself.

The world now stands on the brink of the final abyss. Let us all resolve to take all possible practical steps to ensure that we do not, through our own folly, go over the edge.

THIS ULTIMATE THREAT
Omar N. Bradley

The central problem of our time — as I view it — is how to employ human intelligence for the salvation of mankind. It is a problem we have put upon ourselves. For we have defiled our intellect by the creation of such scientific instruments of destruction that we are now in desperate danger of destroying ourselves. Our plight is critical and with each effort we have made to relieve it by further scientific advance, we have succeeded only in aggravating our peril.

As a result, we are now speeding inexorably toward a day when even the ingenuity of our scientists may be unable to save us from the consequences of a single rash act or a lone reckless hand upon the switch of an uninterceptible missile. For twelve years, we've sought to stave off this ultimate threat of disaster by devising arms which would be both ultimate and disastrous.

This irony can probably be compounded a few more years, or perhaps even a few decades. Missiles will bring antimissiles, and antimissiles will bring antiantimissiles. But inevitably, this whole electronic house of cards will reach a point where it can be constructed no higher.

At that point we shall have come to the peak of this whole incredible dilemma into which the world is shoving itself. And when that time comes, there will be

Omar N. Bradley was the last surviving five-star general of the U.S. Army. He died in 1981. These are excerpts from a talk he gave at a convocation at St. Alban's School, Washington, D.C., 5 November 1957.

little we can do other than to settle down uneasily, smother our fears, and attempt to live in a thickening shadow of death.

Should this situation come to pass, we would have but one single and thin thread to cling to. We call it rationale or reason. We reason that no government, no single group of men — indeed, not even one willful individual — would be so foolhardy, so reckless, as to precipitate a war which would most surely end in mutual destruction.

This reasoning may have the benefit of logic. But even logic sometimes goes awry. How can we assume that reason will prevail in a crisis when there is ordinarily so little reason among people? To those who would take comfort in the likelihood of an atomic peace to be secured solely by rationale and reason, I would recall the lapse of reason in a bunker under the Reich Chancellery in Berlin. It failed before, it can fail again.

Have we already gone too far in this search for peace through the accumulation of peril? Is there any way to halt this trend — or must we push on with new devices until we inevitably come to judgment before the atom? I believe there is a way out. And I believe it because I have acquired in my lifetime a decent respect for human intelligence.

It may be that the problems of accommodation in a world split by rival ideologies are more difficult than those with which we have struggled in the construction of ballistics missiles. But I believe, too, that if we apply to these human problems the energy, creativity, and the perseverance we have devoted to science, even problems of accommodation will yield to reason. Admittedly, the problem of peaceful accommodation in the world is infinitely more difficult than the conquest of space, infinitely more complex than a trip to the moon. But if we will only come to the realization that it must be worked out — whatever it may mean even to such sacred traditions as absolute national sovereignty — I believe that we can somehow, somewhere, and perhaps through some as yet undiscovered world thinker and leader, find a workable solution.

I confess that this is as much an article of faith as it is an expression of reason. But this is what we need — faith in our ability to do what must be done. Without that faith we shall never get started. And until we get started, we shall never know what can be done.

If I am sometimes discouraged, it is not by the magnitude of the problem, but by our colossal indifference to it. I am unable to understand why — if we are willing to trust in reason as a restraint on the use of a ready-made ready-to-fire bomb — we do not make greater, more diligent and more imaginative use of reason and human intelligence in seeking an accord and compromise which will make it possible for mankind to control the atom and banish it as an instrument of war.

This is the ready and — indeed — the most strenuous challenge to human intellect today. By comparison with it, the conquest of space is of small significance. For until we learn how to live together, until we rid ourselves of the strife that mocks our pretensions of civilization, our adventures in science — instead of producing human progress — we will continue to crowd it with greater peril.

We can compete with Sputnik [Sputnik I and II had been launched on Oct. 4 and Nov. 2, 1957] and probably create bigger and better Sputniks of our own. But what are we doing to prevent Sputnik from evolving into just one more weapons system? And when are we going to muster an intelligence equal to that applied against the Sputnik and dedicate it to the preservation of this satellite on which we live?

When does humanity run out?

FAREWELL ADDRESS
Dwight D. Eisenhower

Three days from now, after half a century in the service of our country, I shall lay down the responsibilities of office as, in traditional and solemn ceremony, the authority of the Presidency is vested in my successor.

This evening I come to you with a message of leave-taking and farewell, and to share a few final thoughts with you, my countrymen.

Like every other citizen, I wish the new President, and all who will labor with him, Godspeed. I pray that the coming years will be blessed with peace and prosperity for all.

Our people expect their President and the Congress to find essential agreement on issues of great moment, the wise resolution of which will better shape the future of the nation.

My own relations with the Congress, which began on a remote and tenuous basis when, long ago, a member of the Senate appointed me to West Point, have since ranged to the intimate during the war and immediate postwar period, and, finally, to the mutually interdependent during these past eight years.

In this final relationship, the Congress and the Administration have, on most vital issues, cooperated well, to serve the national good rather than mere partisanship, and so have assured that the business of the nation should go forward. So, my official relationship with the Congress ends in a feeling, on my part, of gratitude that we have been able to do so much together.

We now stand ten years past the midpoint of a century that has witnessed four major wars among great nations. Three of these involved our own country. Despite these holocausts America is today the strongest, the most influential and most productive nation in the world. Understandably proud of this preeminence, we yet realize that America's leadership and prestige depend not merely upon our unmatched material progress, riches, and military strength, but on how we use our power in the interests of world peace and human betterment.

Throughout America's adventure in free government, our basic purposes have been to keep the peace, to foster progress in human achievement, and to enhance liberty, dignity, and integrity among people and among nations. To strive for less would be unworthy of a free and religious people. Any failure traceable to arrogance, or our lack of comprehension or readiness to sacrifice, would inflict upon us grievous hurt both at home and abroad.

President Eisenhower's farewell address was delivered on 17 January 1961.

Progress toward these noble goals is persistently threatened by the conflict now engulfing the world. It commands our whole attention, absorbs our very beings. We face a hostile ideology — global in scope, atheistic in character, ruthless in purpose, and insidious in method. Unhappily the danger it poses promises to be of indefinite duration. To meet it successfully, there is called for, not so much the emotional and transitory sacrifices of crisis, but rather those which enable us to carry forward steadily, surely, and without complaint the burdens of a prolonged and complex struggle — with liberty the stake. Only thus shall we remain, despite every provocation, on our charted course toward permanent peace and human betterment.

Crises there will continue to be. In meeting them, whether foreign or domestic, great or small, there is a recurring temptation to feel that some spectacular and costly action could become the miraculous solution to all current difficulties. A huge increase in newer elements of our defense; development of unrealistic programs to cure every ill in agriculture; a dramatic expansion in basic and applied research — these and many other possibilities, each possibly promising in itself, may be suggested as the only way to the road we wish to travel.

But each proposal must be weighed in the light of a broader consideration: the need to maintain balance in and among national programs — balance between the private and the public economy, balance between cost and hoped for advantage — balance between the clearly necessary and the comfortably desirable; balance between our essential requirements as a nation and the duties imposed by the nation upon the individual; balance between actions of the moment and the national welfare of the future. Good judgment seeks balance and progress; lack of it eventually finds imbalance and frustration.

The record of many decades stands as proof that our people and their government have, in the main, understood these truths and have responded to them well, in the face of stress and threat. But threats, new in kind or degree, constantly arise. I mention two only.

A vital element in keeping the peace is our military establishment. Our arms must be mighty, ready for instant action, so that no potential aggressor may be tempted to risk his own destruction.

Our military organization today bears little relation to that known by any of my predecessors in peacetime, or indeed by the fighting men of World War II or Korea.

Until the latest of our world conflicts, the United States had no armaments industry. American makers of plowshares could, with time and as required, make swords as well. But now we can no longer risk emergency improvisation of national defense; we have been compelled to create a permanent armaments industry of vast proportions. Added to this, three and a half million men and women are directly engaged in the defense establishment. We annually spend on military security more than the net income of all U.S. corporations.

This conjunction of an immense military establishment and a large arms industry is new in the American experience. The total influence — economic, political, even spiritual — is felt in every city, every state house, every office of the federal government. We recognize the imperative need for this development. Yet we must not fail to comprehend its grave implications. Our toil, resources, and livelihood are all involved; so is the very structure of our society.

In the councils of government, we must guard against the acquisition of unwarranted influence, whether sought or unsought, by the military-industrial complex. The potential for the disastrous rise of misplaced power exists and will persist.

We must never let the weight of this combination endanger our liberties or democratic processes. We should take nothing for granted. Only an alert and knowledgeable citizenry can compel the proper meshing of the huge industrial and military machinery of defense with our peaceful methods and goals, so that security and liberty may prosper together.

Akin to, and largely responsible for the sweeping changes in our industrial-military posture, has been the technological revolution during recent decades. In this revolution, research has become central; it also becomes more formalized, complex, and costly. A steadily increasing share is conducted for, by, or at the direction of, the federal government.

Today, the solitary inventor, tinkering in his shop, has been overshadowed by task forces of scientists in laboratories and testing fields. In the same fashion, the free university, historically the fountainhead of free ideas and scientific discovery, has experienced a revolution in the conduct of research. Partly because of the huge costs involved, a government contract becomes virtually a substitute for intellectual curiosity. For every old blackboard there are now hundreds of new electronic computers.

The prospect of domination of the nation's scholars by federal employment, project allocations, and the power of money is ever present — and is gravely to be regarded.

Yet, in holding scientific research and discovery in respect, as we should, we must also be alert to the equal and opposite danger that public policy could itself become the captive of a scientific-technological elite.

It is the task of statesmanship to mold, to balance, and to integrate these and other forces, new and old, within the principles of our democratic system — ever aiming toward the supreme goals of our free society.

Another factor in maintaining balance involves the element of time. As we peer into society's future, we — you and I, and our government — must avoid the impulse to live only for today, plundering, for our own ease and convenience, the precious resources of tomorrow. We cannot mortgage the material assets of our grandchildren without risking the loss also of their political and spiritual heritage. We want democracy to survive for all generations to come, not to become the insolvent phantom of tomorrow.

Down the long lane of history yet to be written America knows that this world of ours, ever growing smaller, must avoid becoming a community of dreadful fear and hate, and be, instead, a proud confederation of mutual trust and respect.

Such a confederation must be one of equals. The weakest must come to the conference table with the same confidence as do we, protected as we are by our moral, economic, and military strength. That table, though scarred by many past frustrations, cannot be abandoned for the certain agony of the battlefield.

Disarmament, with mutual honor and confidence, is a continuing imperative. Together we must learn how to compose differences, not with arms, but with intellect and decent purpose. Because this need is so sharp and apparent I confess that I lay down my official responsibilities in this field with a definite sense of disappointment. As one who has witnessed the horror and the lingering sadness of war — as one who knows that another war could utterly destroy this civilization which has been so slowly and painfully built over thousands of years — I wish I could say tonight that a lasting peace is in sight.

Happily, I can say that war has been avoided. Steady progress toward our ultimate goal has been made. But, so much remains to be done. As a private citizen, I shall never cease to do what little I can to help the world advance along that road.

So — in this my last good-night to you as your President — I thank you for the many opportunities you have given me for public service in war and peace. I trust that in that service you find some ways to improve performance in the future.

You and I — my fellow citizens — need to be strong in our faith that all nations, under God, will reach the goal of peace with justice. May we be ever unswerving in devotion to principle, confident but humble with power, diligent in pursuit of the nation's great goals.

To all the peoples of the world, I once more give expression to America's prayerful and continuing aspiration:

We pray that peoples of all faiths, all races, all nations, may have their great human needs satisfied; that those now denied opportunity shall come to enjoy it to the full; that all who yearn for freedom may experience its spiritual blessings; that those who have freedom will understand, also, its heavy responsibilities; that all who are insensitive to the needs of others will learn charity; that the scourges of poverty, disease, and ignorance will be made to disappear from the earth, and that, in the goodness of time, all peoples will come to live together in a peace guaranteed by the binding force of mutual respect and love.

A Selection from the
FAREWELL ADDRESS
Jimmy Carter

For a few minutes now, I want to lay aside my role as leader of one nation, and speak to you as a fellow citizen of the world about three issues, three difficult issues: the threat of nuclear destruction, our stewardship of the physical resources of our planet, and the preeminence of the basic rights of human beings.

It's now been thirty-five years since the first atomic bomb fell on Hiroshima. The great majority of the world's people cannot remember a time when the nuclear shadow did not hang over the Earth. Our minds have adjusted to it, as after a time our eyes adjust to the dark.

President Carter's farewell address was delivered on 14 January 1981.

Yet the risk of a nuclear conflagration has not lessened. It has not happened yet, thank God, but that can give us little comfort — for it only has to happen once.

The danger is becoming greater. As the arsenals of the superpowers grow in size and sophistication, and as other governments acquire these weapons, it may only be a matter of time before madness, desperation, greed, or miscalculation lets loose this terrible force.

In an all-out nuclear war, more destructive power than in all of World War II would be unleashed every second during the long afternoon it would take for all the missiles and bombs to fall. A World War II every second — more people killed in the first few hours than all the wars of history put together. The survivors, if any, would live in despair amid the poisoned ruins of a civilization that had committed suicide.

National weakness — real or perceived — can tempt aggression and thus cause war. That's why the United States cannot neglect its military strength. We must and we will remain strong. But with equal determination, the United States and all countries must find ways to control and reduce the horrifying danger that is posed by the world's enormous stockpiles of nuclear arms.

This has been a concern of every American President since the moment we first saw what these weapons could do. Our leaders will require our understanding and our support as they grapple with this difficult but crucial challenge. There is no disagreement on the goals or the basic approach to controlling this enormous destructive force. The answer lies not just in the attitudes or actions of world leaders, but in the concern and demands of all of us as we continue our struggle to preserve the peace.

Nuclear weapons are an expression of one side of our human character. But there is another side. The same rocket technology that delivers nuclear warheads has also taken us peacefully into space. From that perspective, we see our Earth as it really is — a small and fragile and beautiful blue globe, the only home we have. We see no barriers of race or religion or country. We see the essential unity of our species and our planet; and with faith and common sense, that bright vision will ultimately prevail.

THE DEFENSE WORKER'S DILEMMA
William W. Winpisinger

In spite of the current trillion-dollar escalation of the military budget, defense workers are more than reluctant to accept what ordinarily would be considered a bonanza.

In the first place, there are implicit moral considerations which lead them to reject military escalation at the expense of great segments of people forced, through no cause of their own, to rely on government assistance and subsistence programs.

William W. Winpisinger is president of the International Association of Machinists and Aerospace workers.

Secondly, the Russians don't appear to be coming — they're mired-down in Afghanistan; can't quell the Polish Solidarity movement; are forced to aim at least a third of their military apparatus toward a hostile China to the East; can't afford to alienate Moslem nations to the South; and have to play expensive military chess with NATO nations to the West.

Third, defense workers, like all but the very wealthiest of citizens, are required to give up a large percentage of their income in the form of taxes — and the currently programmed $1.5 trillion military budget over the next five years means a typical four-person working family is going to pay an average Pentagon tax ranging from $12,000 to $27,000, depending upon where one lives, to pay for it. That's a high price to pay to keep a job.

Fourth, defense workers around the country are now almost fully aware that enormous military expenditures aren't very effective in terms of job security. Military production is capital intensive, not labor intensive, for all but the highly trained and skilled. One billion federal dollars spent anywhere in the civilian sector of the economy — and most notably in those public-service sectors suffering budgetary cutbacks and industrial sectors starved for capital — will create on the average about 30,000 more public-sector jobs and 14,000 more jobs in private industry than does $1 billion worth of military spending.

Additionally, several billions of each year's military budget is used to put defense workers out of work through the introduction of labor-serving new technology. In this sense, the defense worker's Pentagon tax is being used to pay for elimination of his job! Not much economic security in that arrangement — or long-run incentive to work in the industry.

This is why the Machinists, and a number of other unions, have been pressing for an Economic Conversion Program that will remove workers and whole communities from dependency on the Pentagon and the prospect of war.

Perhaps the best way to comprehend the defense worker's dilemma and to grasp the concept of Economic Conversion, is to simulate what happens when military production ceases for any of a number of reasons — even in times of escalating military budgets.

Rumor of Weapon Able's demise has, let us suppose, been rife for five years. Workers and community officials have trembled at the prospect. But each time, employers and employees, labor and management, city officials and civic leaders have petitioned Congressman Jones and Senator Smith, who have taken the case to the Pentagon, and each time the funds have been restored. Weapon Able has always come through.

This year, however, Congressman Jones and Senator Smith failed in their mission of mercy. It is now conclusive: the Pentagon insists that the Russians have developed Weapon Counter-Able, making Weapon Able totally obsolete. A new weapon is demanded, wholly different in design, matrix and purpose. Baker, Inc., which makes Weapon Able at its Caltex plant, finds that facility is obsolete too. So are the subcontractor plants and component manufacturing plants.

At this point, panic seizes workers and whole communities. Baker, Inc. could decide to convert its Caltex plant into production of civilian products but there are other considerations. The company has decided it no longer cares to do business in Caltex. The plant has been wholly depreciated and has no further tax advantages. The unions there negotiated solid contracts over the years and wage and benefit levels are at or above those of Baker plants located elsewhere, primarily in the Sunbelt, producing other weapons and products. In fact, Baker, Inc. management figures the damned union is too strong. It's about time it was broken up.

However one looks at it, Baker, Inc. stands to profit by giving up operations in Caltex. And that's what private enterprise is all about: maximizing profits.

Individually, defense workers may fervently hope and wish for peace, for scaling down the arms race, for an end to the international trafficking in arms. They may want to support SALT agreements and nuclear-nonproliferation treaties and restrict arms sales.

Yet for them to support those laudable objectives demands a nobility of spirit and a courage of self-sacrifice that are asked of no other members of society, except those who are called and serve during actual wartime. It is an excruciating dilemma and it makes absolutely no sense — economically, politically, or socially. But before we come to that, consider the typical situation.

The Pentagon announces that Weapon Able production is to be halted. Baker, Inc. has been the prime contractor for fifteen years, employing some 5,000 workers to produce Weapon Able at its Caltex plant. Subcontracting firms in two other communities employ another 5,000 people who work at jobs directly related to Weapon Able. At the third tier, a half-dozen firms scattered around the country employ in all 3,500 people to manufacture component parts for the device. In addition, a dozen vendor firms and service suppliers have been directly dependent on the Weapon Able contract; that's a few thousand more people. And in the community of Caltex, as in the dozen or so other communities where subcontractors, component manufacturers, vendor and service suppliers may be located, Weapon Able has an immediate economic bearing on the full spectrum of local economic activity and public finance. In all, 15,000 or more people are directly affected by the fate of Weapon Able, and countless others concerned in varying degree.

For its part, the company was cleverly able to write into its prime contract with the Pentagon that, should Weapon Able's production be curtailed, the U.S. Government would indemnify Baker, Inc. for loss of the contract and production. The indemnity would amount to an average of the profits derived in the best five years of Able production, and would cover a two-year "economic adjustment" period. That indemnity payment would come to $10 million. No severe dilemma there.

But, back in Caltex and a dozen other Weapon Able communities, workers are laid off. Unemployment insurance claim lines are long, but the workers will receive two-thirds of the state's average weekly wage for twenty-six weeks. If, after that time, they still haven't found work, they may get a thirteen-week extension of unemployment benefits.

The community fathers, businessmen, and civic leaders rally somewhat from their initial shock. They form a local industrial development committee and hire a full-time director to (1) write federal grant applications for economic development assistance; and (2) scout and recruit prospective firms to buy or lease the Weapon Able plant and start producing widgets. The latter chore is called Operation Bootstrap.

Months pass, with the national unemployment rate hanging high at near 8 percent; in Caltex, it is now 14 percent. But undaunted, the local real estate broker comes up with an idea to level the old Weapon Able building, subdivide the ten-acre tract and sell lots for new condominiums, even though mortgage loan defaults are at an all-time high. The Chamber of Commerce proposes, instead, a city-financed industrial park. Its promotional literature stresses the advantages of a "free labor market" and assorted tax giveaways as tax lures for businesses. Local bankers suggest selling industrial development bonds, rather than directly charging local taxpayers for the park.

Unemployment compensation for the laid-off defense workers had expired after thirty-nine weeks. Therefore, when it was learned that Baker, Inc. had gone overseas and was now producing Weapon Able in Gomorrah, to secure that nation's defense against its arch rival, Sodom, the workers' international union applied for Trade Adjustment Assistance, which prior to Reagan budget slashes, would have given them a two-year lease on life at 75 percent of pay. However, the Labor Department ruled that the loss of their jobs was unrelated to foreign trade.

After about a year, the Department of Defense's Office of Economic Adjustment announces it has approved a $20,000 grant to survey the Caltex community and estimate its needs. The dozen other Weapon Able communities are not included in the survey; DOD's OEA lacks the money to assist every defense impacted community. And there's a little hitch at Caltex. OEA has asked the Economic Development Administration's Title IX section to administer the grant, but EDA's Title IX funds have always been nearly nonexistent and the Reagan budget priority is to eliminate EDA altogether.

Anyone remotely familiar with declining communities, whether in the agricultural Midwest, the heart of New York City, or under the leaden skies of New England, can finish the scenario. There is no happy ending to this tale of economic and social woe.

Several conclusions can be drawn from this fictitious but unexaggerated story of Weapon Able. The point that must first be recognized is that, until the fears of the nation's 2.5 million defense production workers in private industry can be constructively alleviated and their employment security assured, it may well be impossible to consider arms and military control measures and the defense budget on their merits. Indeed, since the economic recession of 1974–75, the ever-escalating Pentagon budget has more and more been sold as a giant public-works program, and less and less as an essential and rational national defense program.

Second, chronically high levels of unemployment aid and abet the cause of the Pentagon's big spenders. It is too much to expect that congressmen and senators will support defense budget cuts and resist extravagant and unnecessary weapons procurement programs when the unemployment rate in their states or districts stands at punishing levels.

Third, private enterprise cannot be trusted to relieve defense workers and their communities of their dilemma. Profit maximization does not run in tandem with either full employment or continuity of employment. Free-market dogma does not fit the defense industry, since it is wholly dependent on direct federal expenditures for both production and research-and-development contracts. Competition is extremely slight in the industry.

It is both monopolistic and monopsonistic, but that isn't deterring corporate contractors and the Pentagon from demanding that Congress remove the last vestiges of profit controls and regulatory safeguards from military production — while opposing economic safeguards for workers and communities.

It is fair to ask, however, when the military production contract expires, whether defense firms — particularly large, prime contractors of the multinational stripe — have any moral, economic, or social responsibilities to the workers and communities whom they've enlisted (drafted may be more appropriate) in serving the national interest for profit? Shouldn't society expect from business at least the same things business expects from the community and its workers — namely dependability, stability, and fairness?

But if private business is to be absolved from accepting those responsibilities, then clearly the federal government has a duty to meet them. Defense work is required by the government in the name of the national interest. If it then curtails that work, it has a responsibility to pass measures and shape programs to make sure that workers and whole communities do not suffer as a consequence.

That is where Planned Economic Conversion comes in.

Simply put, Planned Economic Conversion is a method to convert defense plant, equipment, and workers to socially useful peacetime production. Beyond this, conceptual refinements are necessary. Planned Economic Conversion requires that notification be given in advance of an impending cutback or shutdown, so that a conversion plan can be developed before the ax falls. It requires, further, an assessment of local community needs and it requires stimulation of demand for civilian production by the declaration of a backlog of public needs.

Railroad rehabilitation, mass-transit construction and manufacture, development of solar energy and other alternative energy sources, low-cost housing and solid-waste recycling plants are critical and long-neglected public needs. Government-sponsored manufacture of the industrial goods necessary to meet them is the obvious key to successful economic conversion. These new industries would be located in those plants and communities crippled by defense cutbacks.

In fact, a six-point safe renewable energy conservation and energy conversion program would, for the ten-year projected cost of the MX missile program, eliminate unemployment totally and enhance our national security by getting us off the cartelized OPEC-Seven Sister oil import book.

After thirty years of spiraling arms competition, it is evident that the only true guarantee of national security is a balanced foreign policy and a strong, diversified civilian economy operating at full employment. Defense spending can be cut back. With proper advanced planning, our national security and economic vitality will not be imperiled by that prudent step. On the contrary, they will be enhanced. Therefore, Economic Conversion must become a viable component of national security strategy.

DEVELOPMENT AND THE ARMS RACE
Robert S. McNamara

The old order is certainly passing. Perhaps the beginning of its breakdown can be dated from that cold December day in 1942 when a few hundred yards from where we are now sitting the first nuclear chain reaction began. The consequences of that event were to transform our whole concept of international security because now man had the capacity not merely to wage war, but to destroy civilization itself.

If I may on this occasion speak quite personally, I had of course to wrestle with the problem of the fundamental nature of international security during my tenure as U.S. Secretary of Defense, and in 1966 I spoke publicly about it in a speech to the American Society of Newspaper Editors meeting in Montreal.

My central point was that the concept of security itself had become dangerously oversimplified. There had long been an almost universal tendency to think of the security problem as being exclusively a military problem, and to think of the military problem as being primarily a weapons-system or hardware problem.

"We still tend to conceive of national security," I noted, "almost solely as a state of armed readiness: a vast, awesome arsenal of weaponry."

But, I pointed out, if one reflects on the problem more deeply, it is clear that force alone does not guarantee security, and that a nation can reach a point at which it does not buy more security for itself simply by buying more military hardware.

That was my view then. It remains my view now.

Let me be precise about this point.

No nation can avoid the responsibility of providing an appropriate and reasonable level of defense for its society. In an imperfect world that is necessary. But what is just as necessary is to understand that the concept of security encompasses far more than merely military force, and that a society can reach a point at which additional military expenditure no longer provides additional security.

Indeed, to the extent that such expenditure severely reduces the resources available for other essential sectors and social services — and fuels a futile and reactive arms race — excessive military spending can erode security rather than enhance it.

Many societies today are facing that situation. Certainly the world as a

Robert S. McNamara is a former U.S. Secretary of Defense and President of the World Bank. His remarks were taken from an address made at the University of Chicago 22 May 1979, upon receiving the Albert Pick, Jr., Award.

whole is. And any sensible way out of the problem must begin with the realization of the dangers and disproportionate costs that extravagant military spending imposes on human welfare and social progress.

Global defense expenditures have grown so large that it is difficult to grasp their full dimensions. The overall total is now in excess of $400 billion a year.

An estimated 36 million men are under arms in the world's active regular and paramilitary forces, with another 25 million in reserves, and some 30 million civilians in military-related occupations.

Public expenditures on weapons research and development now approach $30 billion a year, and mobilize the talents of half a million scientists and engineers throughout the world. That is a greater research effort than is devoted to any other activity on earth, and it consumes more public research money than is spent on the problems of energy, health, education, and food combined.

The United States and the Soviet Union together account for more than half of the world's total defense bill, and for some two-thirds of the world's arms trade. And yet it is not in the industrialized nations, but in the developing countries, that military budgets are rising the fastest.

On the average around the world, one tax dollar in six is devoted to military expenditure, and that means that at present levels of spending the average taxpayer can expect over his lifetime to give up three to four years of his income to the arms race.

And what will he have bought with that? Greater security?

No. At these exaggerated levels, only greater risk, greater danger, and greater delay in getting on with life's real purposes.

It is imperative that we understand this issue clearly. The point is not that a nation's security is relatively less important than other considerations. Security is fundamental. The point is simply that excessive military spending can *reduce* security rather than strengthen it.

In the matter of military force — as in many other matters in life — more is not necessarily better. Beyond a prudent limit, more can turn out to be very much worse. And if we examine defense expenditures around the world today — and measure them realistically against the full spectrum of actions that tend to promote order and stability within and among nations — it is obvious that there is a very irrational misallocation of resources.

Is there any way, then, to moderate the mad momentum of a global arms race?

No very easy way, given the degree of suspicion and distrust involved. But as one who participated in the initial nuclear test ban arrangements, and other arms limitation discussions, I am absolutely convinced that sound workable agreements are attainable. These matters clearly call for realism. But realism is not a hardened, inflexible, unimaginative attitude. On the contrary, the realistic mind should be a restlessly creative mind — free of naive delusions, but full of practical alternatives. There are many alternatives available to an arms race. There are many far better ways of contributing to global security. I suggested a number of those ways in my address in Montreal in 1966, pointing out the importance of accelerating economic and social progress in the developing countries. When, two years later, I left the Pentagon for the World Bank, this was an aspect of world order with which I was particularly concerned.

Eleven years in the Bank, combined with visits to some one hundred of the developing countries, have contributed immeasurably to my international understanding. They have permitted me to explore the whole new world that has come to political independence — in large part over the past quarter century.

I have met the leaders of this new world — their Jeffersons and Washingtons and Franklins — and have sensed their pride and their peoples' pride in their new national independence, and their frustrations at their economic dependence.

I have shared their sense of achievement at the remarkable rate of economic growth which many of them attained, largely by their own efforts. But I have been appalled by the desperate plight of those who did not share in this growth, and whose numbers rose relentlessly with the great tide of population expansion. . . .

The U.S. economy increasingly depends on the ability of the developing nations both to purchase its exports and to supply it with important raw materials.

And the same sort of relationship of mutual interdependence exists between the other industrialized countries — the Common Market, and Japan — and the developing world.

Thus, for the developed nations to do more to assist the developing countries is not merely the right thing to do, it is also increasingly the economically advantageous thing to do.

What will it cost the United States and the other industrialized countries to do more?

Far less than most of us imagine.

The truth is that the developed nations would not have to reduce their already immensely high standard of living in the slightest, but only to devote a minuscule proportion of the additional per capita income they will earn over the coming decade. It is not a question of the rich nations diminishing their present wealth in order to help the poor nations. It is only a question of their being willing to share a tiny percentage — perhaps 3 percent — of their incremental income.

It is true that the developed nations, understandably preoccupied with controlling inflation, and searching for structural solutions to their own economic imbalances, may be tempted to conclude that until these problems are solved, aid considerations must simply be put aside. But support for development is not a luxury — something desirable when times are easy, and superfluous when times become temporarily troublesome.

It is precisely the opposite. Assistance to the developing countries is a continuing social and moral responsibility, and its need now is greater than ever.

Will we live up to that responsibility?

As I look back over my own generation — a generation that in its university years thought of itself as liberal — I am astonished at the insensitivity that all of us had during those years to the injustice of racial discrimination in our own society.

Will it now take another fifty years before we fully recognize the injustice of massive poverty in the international community?

We cannot let that happen.

Nor will it happen — if we but turn our minds seriously to the fundamental issues involved.

Increasingly, the old priorities and the old value judgments are being reexamined in the light of the growing interdependence between nations — and it is right that they should be. Once they are thought through, it will be evident that international development is one of the most important movements underway in this century. It may ultimately turn out to be the most important.

Our task, then, is to explore — to explore a turbulent world that is shifting uneasily beneath our feet even as we try to understand it. And to explore our own values and beliefs about what kind of a world we really want it to become.

NO MIDDLE GROUND: THE DRAFT, NUCLEAR WAR, AND THE JUST WAR THEORY
Nathaniel W. Pierce

There is much unfinished business left over from the war in Vietnam. I sense a need in many people to forget, to pretend that it never happened, to get on with the future and forget the past.

However, we live in a world which will not yield to us that luxury. The current discussion about reestablishing the draft as draft registration continues raises once again the very basic issue of the Christian's relationship with the secular state as it pertains to military service. During the Vietnam era Christian people were deeply divided over this question. Now that much of the emotionalism which surrounded Vietnam has subsided, perhaps we can examine the situation more thoughtfully.

The specific issue which demands immediate attention is the "just war" approach to military service. Most mainline denominations subscribe to this approach. It invites each individual Christian to assess each war on the basis of seven or so criteria, which for the purposes of this article are stated as follows:

1) A just war must be a last resort.

2) A just war must have a noble or good end.

3) A just war must be declared by lawful authority.

4) A just war must have a reasonable prospect of success.

5) A just war must not do more harm than the good which may result; the means used must be proportional, and insofar as possible noncombatants must be protected.

Nathaniel W. Pierce is the rector of Grace Episcopal Church, Nampa, Idaho. He is a past national chairman of the Episcopal Peace Fellowship; a consultant to the World Without War Council in Berkeley, California; and a member of the Joint Commission on Peace of the Episcopal Church.

6) A just war demands just conduct by participants.

7) A just war requires that mercy be shown to those defeated.

The purpose of the "just war" approach is not to bless wars or to declare them righteous, recent past history notwithstanding. Rather, recognizing both the possibility of war and the morally questionable nature of all wars, its purpose is to hedge them about with restrictions, setting forth those criteria necessary before the resort to war can be morally justified and seeking to limit the means that can be morally employed in the actual conduct of even a justifiable war. The intent is to say that only within the most carefully specified limits and in view of the most compelling ends can Christians justify the use of military force or legitimately participate in it themselves.

The roots of this approach go back to the days of St. Augustine and St. Ambrose. The Christian community has refined the criteria ever since to meet changing realities.

Perhaps now, some ten years later, we can see more clearly that the war in Vietnam did not meet *any* of the seven criteria for a just war with the possible exception of number seven. Since we were the defeated, I will leave it up to the reader to decide whether we were treated mercifully by our opponents after the war ended.

As we face the probability of a renewed draft, it is time to rethink our view of the just war theory. Perhaps the most pressing reason for reconsideration is the simple fact that the U.S. Supreme Court has declared this position unlawful.

In addition the possibility of nuclear warfare raises a serious question as to whether any war could conform to the just war criteria.

The Supreme Court decision came as the draft was being phased out in the early 1970s. Louis A. Negre, a Christian, sought to be discharged from the military because of his opposition to the war in Vietnam. His application for discharge was based on his understanding of the just war approach.

His request was denied as war judicial relief by *habeas corpus* in the U.S. District Court. The court of appeals ruled that "Negre objects to the war in Vietnam, not to all wars," and therefore "does not quality for separation (from the Army) as a conscientious objector."

When the case reached the Supreme Court (*Negre* v. *Larsen*) the justices were willing to concede that Negre's decision to apply just war theology to his involvement in the war in Vietnam was motivated by conscience and well-established theological convictions. However, in the words of Justice Thurgood Marshall, who delivered the majority opinion:

> Our analysis shows that the impact of conscription on objectors to particular wars is far from unjustified. The conscription laws, applied to such persons, as to others, are not designed to interfere with any religious ritual or practice, and do not work a penalty against any theological position. The incidental burdens felt by persons in petitioner's position are strictly justified by substantial government interests that relate directly to the very impacts questioned.

Thus, the Supreme Court continued to protect religious ritual and practice, but declared the application of the just war approach to a particular war by a draftee, or by one already serving in the military, to be illegal.

This, of course, presents Christians with a dilemma. The just war approach is still useful in determining whether participation in a particular war can be morally justified. If, however, such analysis should lead to a decision to be a selective conscientious objector to a particular war, we are faced with a government that will not recognize this position. In effect, then, there is no middle ground left. One is either 100 percent willing to serve in the military under any circumstances or 100 percent opposed to serving in the military under any circumstances. To qualify either stance is to become an illegal, selective conscientious objector.

The middle ground has also been eroded although not yet incinerated, by the advent of nuclear weapons. When we consider the seven criteria of the just war approach, how could any nuclear war be rationalized? Can the just war criteria, especially its key principles of "discrimination" and "proportionality" in the conduct of war, have any continuing meaning in a nuclear era? Can nuclear war, and the ever-present possibility that conventional war may escalate into nuclear war, ever be a legitimate expression of the obligation to preserve life or to seek a love-inspired justice in and among nations? How does one show mercy to an annihilated world?

By virtue of its illegality in these United States, and further in view of the impossibility of any nuclear war meeting the just war criteria, we are confronted with a profound choice. Either we seek peace through military strength, thereby running the risk of total and immoral destruction, or we initiate a work for a world without war unprecedented in human history.

It is more than likely that Vietnam was our last conventional war. Our moral justification of that war is now clearly seen to have been empty. It is naive to believe that nuclear arsenals can continue indefinitely to play a major role in the defense policies of the nuclear powers without such weapons eventually being used. No longer may we send our young men to war, comforted by any notion that they may turn their back on immorality.

The middle ground has disintegrated legally and practically, and we are faced with a choice as a Christian community.

DEALING WITH THE DEVIL:
A COST-BENEFIT ANALYSIS
William Sloane Coffin, Jr.

I cannot think of a more bitterly appropriate acronym than the one for "mutually assured destruction." It is MAD, and mad it is. Never credible to the heart, our defense policy now is no more credible to the mind.

William Sloane Coffin, Jr., senior minister of Riverside Church in New York City, has been an army officer, CIA agent, university chaplain, civil rights and antiwar activist.

© *1978 by Christianity and Crisis,* Inc. Reprinted from the 27 November issue.

Here is an analogy. Let us suppose the chief of police of your town announces that the police force has abandoned traditional means of fighting crime and henceforth will rely on deterrence: Whenever a murder is committed, every last one of the murderer's family and friends will be hunted down and summarily executed.

The difference between that insane policy and our system of deterrence vis-a-vis the Soviet Union is a matter of scale. We have announced our intention, should the Soviets strike against us (or perhaps even if we believe they are about to strike), of killing some 200 million Soviet citizens, almost none of whom will have had any more say in any decision to attack us than the family of a murderer has in most killings.

The analogy continues. Most murderers do not *decide* to kill, and if the U.S. and Soviet governments continue to reset the nuclear balance at ever higher levels of terror, it is conceivable that a world-destroying nuclear exchange will occur without conscious human choice. The newest weapons are clearly not designed to provide a lethal retaliatory second strike; we've had that capacity for a long time. By their speed, sophistication, and accuracy, these latest weapons reflect the hope of their designers that somehow, some day, one side or the other will be able to carry out a preemptive first strike that will destroy or badly cripple the opponent's ability to respond in kind. Already it takes an intercontinental ballistic missle (ICBM) less than ten minutes to travel door to door. With the introduction of new and trickier designs, the time will come, as physicist Ralph De Lapp predicts, when both sides will move toward or adopt a "launch upon warning" strategy, and the launch decision will be given over to the impersonal province of the computer.

Picture this scenario: an American computer misreads an American radar screen — they are highly complex mechanisms — and sends our missiles on their way; whereupon a Soviet computer, correctly reading a Soviet radar screen, launches theirs. Somewhere in the Stygian darkness of outer space American missiles descending hurtle past Soviet missiles ascending. Seconds later vast fractions of the populations of both countries are dead or dying — with no one having issued any order.

Why do both the Russians and the Americans (and others as well) go on developing weapons whose threatened use can only further destabilize an already precarious balance? Unfortunately, since Robert McNamara's time at the Department of Defense, no Secretary of Defense, no Secretary of State, and no President, has seen fit seriously to confront the question: How much is enough?

To his credit, McNamara did. He insisted that superiority was not the important criterion, nor for that matter was parity. *Sufficiency* was the only relevant standard. We had to have a retaliatory strike capacity of delivering "unacceptable damage." Such a strike, he thought, could be delivered with 400 EMT ("equivalent megatons"), which he estimated would destroy 30 percent of the Soviet population (not including deaths caused by fall-out and radiation) and 70 percent of Soviet industry. To protect the second-strike capability, McNamara and his aids devised a "triadic" defense, any leg of which would be able to inflict the damage described independently of the other two. In 1967 the three legs were: (1) 1,054 land-based ICBMs in their reinforced concrete silos; (2) 41 submarines, some of them always at sea and operational; and (3) 160 long-range strategic bombers, of which some would always be airborne.

It may sound like — and it was — "megamurder," to use a phrase of Canada's General Burns. But at least the Department of Defense explicitly stated that enough was enough, overkill was overkill, superfluous weapons were just that.

That sense of limits has gone. Since 1967 our supply of death-tipped missiles has risen from enough to wipe out the two hundred largest Soviet cities to a stockpile that translates into a kill power twelve times the world population. And we are building more bombs: three every day. What happened to "sufficiency"? Former Assistant Secretary of Defense Packard has given the answer: "Sufficiency is a damn good word to use in a speech. Beyond that it doesn't mean a goddamned thing."

This escalation may remind readers of another kind. It goes: Smart, smarter, smartest — stupid. There is a corollary: Powerful, more powerful, most powerful — powerless. Right now you and I are powerless to protect our lives and our world; they rest in the care of our fallible leaders and their fallible machines. The nation does still have power to destroy, but — because the offense is always and perhaps inherently more potent than the defense — we are literally defenseless. We have no control over whether nuclear war starts, once it does, nothing can save us. And it *can start.*

Napoleon said: "You can do everything with bayonets except sit on them." That is to say: Bayonets can carve a roast. Bayonets can enforce policy. One must think differently of strategic nuclear weapons. One can do nothing with them except kill everyone. At the dawn of the nuclear age President Truman and the majority of his Cabinet did not see the difference; they thought the nuclear age was merely the extension of the prenuclear age. Truman believed the Bomb could serve the political interests of the state. But today Soviet nuclear weapons can't keep the French out of Africa, nor can ours keep the Cubans out. Since their only possible *use* is to initiate a global massacre, the only function they serve prior to use is to maintain and steadily increase the risk that the massacre will happen.

President Kennedy once said that "the risks in disarmament pale in comparison to the risks inherent in an unlimited arms race." The question is: Why were his words never matched by deeds? Why don't the rest of us realize the truth of his words — or, for that matter, why don't we see the enormous waste, the inflation, the loss of jobs the arms race imposes, the unmet needs it keeps unmet? The middle class is revolting, in these days of Proposition 13, against taxes for schools, welfare, urban maintenance, and renovation. Why does it not turn against the Pentagon?

There are many answers, but I do not believe distrust of the Russians is the most basic. The fundamental reason is suggested in Luke 4, describing the second temptation of Christ: The Devil takes Jesus up to a high place and shows him "all the kingdoms of the world in a moment of time." After claiming that they all belong to him, he offers them to Jesus on the condition that Jesus agree to serve him; to which Jesus replies: "It is written 'The Lord thy God, him only wilt thou serve.' "

The parable can be politicized. Recently I wrote on one side of a sheet of paper: "Service to the Lord." On the other I wrote: "Service to the Devil." I was asking: What is the one thing you could not give up if you were serious about serving God or serving the Devil? Following St. Paul, it seemed obvious that if you have not love you have nothing to offer in the service of God. It was less clear what the "one thing necessary" might be for service to the Devil, but the temptation in the Lukan story suggests an answer: Power — seeking status through power. And it seems to me that the Devil has taken us Americans to a high place and, after showing us all the kingdoms of the world in a moment of time, is proposing we can control them all, be preeminent over all, but only if we are willing to destroy them all, or at least to run that risk forevermore.

And we are listening. We are indeed willing to keep our own lives and the lives of all people hostage to chance rather than abandon our meaningless and useless military predominance. "We're number one!" our President told a Texas audience, "and we're going to stay that way." In our hearts we repeat the chant as mindlessly as the fans of a winning World Series team. In terms of military strength we are the Hertz of the world, and we are proud of it. Let Avis try harder; they'll never catch up. Our "pride-swollen faces have closed up our eyes." Or, as Ezekiel laments over Tyre, "You have corrupted your wisdom for the sake of your splendor."

More than anything else, it is this irrational love of loveless power that keeps us in avid pursuit of illusory aims, that drives us to maximize military strength in the most dangerous of ways rather than to try to create a new basis for our security. It is a myth that preparation for war will lead to peace. The proper analogy is not to be found in the story of an armed Hitler and a disarmed Europe. We should dwell instead on 1914, when arms for "defense" and "deterrence" in reality precipitated, accelerated and expanded the grisly proceedings of World War I — and when insistence on total victory, on utter humiliation and harsh punishment of the defeated "Huns" prepared the way for Nazi revanchism.

It is a myth that human power is self-justifying. The truth is that power is justified only by the proper uses to which it is put. It is a myth that biblical religion sanctifies power. The truth is that it unmasks and delegitimizes power. And it is true that indifference to evil is the worst of evils.

SCIENCE AND CONSCIENCE
Pope John Paul II

At Hiroshima, the facts spoke for themselves, in a way that is dramatic, unforgettable, and unique. In the fact of an unforgettable tragedy, which

Excerpts from an address by Pope John Paul II during a visit to Hiroshima, Japan, on 25 February 1981.

touches us all as human beings, how can we fail to express our brotherhood and our deep sympathy at the frightful wound inflicted on the cities of Japan that bear the names of Hiroshima and Nagasaki?

That wound affected the whole of the human family. Hiroshima and Nagasaki: few events in history have had such an effect on man's conscience. The representatives of the world of science were not the ones least affected by the moral crisis caused throughout the world by the explosion of the first atomic bomb. The human mind had in fact made a terrible discovery. We realized with horror that nuclear energy would henceforth be available as a weapon of devastation; then we learned that this terrible weapon had in fact been used, for the first time, for military purposes. And then there arose the question that will never leave us again: Will this weapon, perfected and multiplied beyond measure, be used tomorrow? If so, would it not probably destroy the human family?

In a number of countries, associations of scholars and research workers express the anxiety of the scientific world in the face of an irresponsible use of science, which too often does grievous damage to the balance of nature, or brings with it the ruin and oppression of man by man. . . . Criticism of science and technology is sometimes so severe that it comes close to condemning science itself. On the contrary, science and technology are a wonderful product of a God-given human creativity, since they have provided us with wonderful possibilities, and we all gratefully benefit from them. But we know that this potential is not a neutral one: it can be used either for man's progress or for his degradation. . . .

In the past, it was possible to destroy a village, a town, a region, even a country. Now, it is the whole planet that has come under threat. This fact should finally compel everyone to face a basic moral consideration: from now on, it is only through a conscious choice and through a deliberate policy that humanity can survive. The moral and political choice that faces us is that of putting all the resources of mind, science, and culture at the service of peace and of the building-up of a new society, a society that will succeed in eliminating the causes of fratricidal wars by generously pursuing the total progress of each individual and of all humanity. Of course, individuals and societies are always exposed to the passions of greed and hate; but, as far as within us lies, let us try effectively to correct the social situations and structures that cause injustice and conflict. We shall build peace by building a more humane world. In the light of this hope, the scientific, cultural, and university world has an eminent part to play. Peace is one of the loftiest achievements of culture, and for this reason it deserves all our intellectual and spiritual energy. . . .

Our future on this planet, exposed as it is to nuclear annihilation, depends upon one single factor: humanity must make a moral about-face. At the present moment of history, there must be a general mobilization of all men and women of goodwill. Humanity is being called upon to take a major step forward, a step forward in civilization and wisdom. A lack of civilization, an ignorance of man's true values, brings the risk that humanity will be destroyed. We must become wiser. . . .

The people of our time possess, in the first place, tremendous scientific and technological resources. And we are convinced that these resources could be far more effectively used for the development and growth of peoples. Let us envisage the progress made in agriculture, biology, medicine, and the social communications media applied to education; then there are the social and economic sciences, and the science of planning — all of which could combine to direct in a more humane and effective way the process of industrialization and urbanization, and promote the new models of international cooperation. If all the rich nations of the world wanted to, they could call in an impressive number of specialists for the tasks of development. All of this obviously presupposes political choices, and, more fundamentally, moral options. The moment is approaching when priorities will have to be redefined. For example, it has been estimated that about a half of the world's research workers are at present employed for military purposes. Can the human family morally go on much longer in this direction?

There is also the question of the economic resources needed for giving a decisive impulse to the integral advancement of the human family. Here, too, we are faced with choices. Can we remain passive when we are told that humanity spends immensely more money on arms than on development, and when we learn that one soldier's equipment costs many times more than a child's education? . . .

Science and technology are the most dynamic factors in the development of society today, but their intrinsic limitations do not make them capable, by themselves, of providing a power that will bind culture together. How then can a culture absorb science and technology, with their dynamism, without losing its own identity?

There are three temptations to be avoided in this regard. The *first* is the temptation to pursue technological development for its own sake, the sort of development that has for its only norm that of its own growth and affirmation, as if it were a matter of an independent reality in between nature and a reality that is properly human, imposing on man the inevitable realization of his ever new possibilities, as if one should always do what is technically possible. The *second* temptation is that of subjecting technological development to economic usefulness in accordance with the logic of profit or nonstop economic expansion, thus creating advantages for some while leaving others in poverty, with no care for the true common good of humanity, making technology into an instrument at the service of the ideology of "having." *Third,* there is also the temptation to subject technological development to the pursuit or maintenance of power, as happens when it is used for military purposes.

I urge all scientists, centers of research, and universities to study more deeply the ethical problems of the technological society, a subject that is already engaging the attention of a number of modern thinkers. It is a question that is closely connected with the problem of the just sharing of resources, the use of techniques for peaceful purposes, the development of nations. . . .

In a word, I believe that our generation is faced by a great moral challenge, one which consists in harmonizing the values of science with the values of conscience. Speaking to UNESCO on 2 June 1980, I made an appeal that I put before you again.

> A conviction, which is at the same time a moral imperative, forces itself upon anyone who has become aware of the situation . . . consciences must be mobilized! The efforts of human consciences must be increased in proportion to the tension between good and evil to which people at the end of the twentieth century are subjected. We must convince ourselves of the priority of ethics over technology, of the primacy of the person over things, of the superiority of the spirit over matter. . . ."

PEACEMAKING AND SACRAMENTAL INTEGRITY
William C. Frey

It is my thesis that if the Christian church is to celebrate with any integrity the two principle sacraments of the Gospel — Baptism and the Eucharist — she must be actively engaged in the work of peacemaking and of feeding the hungry.

Baptism, union with Christ Jesus, means the incorporation of people of many languages, nations, and tribes into a single new humanity where the old national, social, economic, and even sexual barriers are eliminated. "For as many of you as were baptized into Christ have put on Christ. There is neither Jew nor Greek, there is neither slave nor free, there is neither male nor female; for you are all one in Christ Jesus." (Galatians 3:27–28)

The Eucharist — the Lord's Supper — is, among many other things, the Lord's way of feeding the hungry, of providing his people with food which they desperately need but cannot manufacture. And as Paul pointed out so eloquently to the Corinthians, worthy participation must involve an active concern for the poor and hungry. "When you meet together, it is not the Lord's Supper that you eat. For in eating, each one goes ahead with his own meal, and one is hungry and another is drunk. What! . . . Do you despise the Church of God, humiliate those who have nothing? . . . For anyone who eats and drinks without discerning the body eats and drinks judgment upon himself." (I Corinthians 11:20–22; 29)

Baptism is a great deal more than simply "doing the baby." It is participation in Christ's work of reconciling all things to himself. And the Eucharist is far more than simply "saying Mass." It is participation in Christ's work of feeding the hungry, not with cheap bread made from stones, but with the shared bread which fed the multitudes with loaves and fishes blessed by his hand.

Without such understanding, both Baptism and the Eucharist are easily

William C. Frey is Episcopal bishop of Colorado and chairman of the Joint Commission on Peace of the General Convention of the Episcopal Church.

reduced from the status of true sacraments to quaint but ultimately meaning-less cultic practices. There is an urgency in this. If the Christian proclamation is to have any authenticity, we must energetically cultivate visible links be-tween the sacramental and the societal aspects of our faith.

But there is an urgency from another side as well, and I suspect that we Christians may not be aware of the dimensions of the emergency which we are facing. Or if we are, we may not know what to do about it. The level of violence in our society has reached epidemic levels, but the Church of Jesus Christ is by and large silent, or at best, selectively vocal. Christian faith in the resurrec-tion can easily give us a cavalier attitude toward death, but if we are not careful it could at the same time obscure our responsibility as faithful stewards of God's creation.

My years in Latin America brought me face to face with violence of many different kinds, and forced me to reflect on it not only sociologically and politically, but theologically and biblically as well. There was the violence of guerrilla warfare and revolution, the violence of repression and terrorism by military regimes, the violence of kidnapping, torture, and assassination. There was the institutionalized violence of a society where life was counted cheap, and economic privilege was universally sought and savagely protected. There was the violence of the right and the violence of the left.

If I learned anything from my experiences and reflections, it was the simple truth that violence begets violence, and that when the Bible says that we must not render evil for evil but rather overcome evil with good, it is not engaging in religious rhetoric but simply describing one of the immutable laws of the universe. Violence, whatever the cause, injures and dehumanizes both its victim and its agent, and what is not often understood, has the power to harden the hearts and erode the sensibilities of those we like to call the innocent bystand-ers. The unnatural and the unthinkable can gradually come to be taken for granted in a violent society.

Few things in recent years have helped me to see this danger with greater clarity than a remark by a young man, quoted recently in one of the Sunday supplement magazines of a Denver newspaper. The young man worked in a missile silo. The reporter questioned him about the tensions caused by living in such a high-pressure environment where at any moment one might be called upon to turn the keys and press the buttons that would annihilate a large portion of the human race. He then asked the young man about the attrition rate; how many people resigned because of the pressure and the tension? And the young man replied that indeed there were a few who did resign. "They just can't handle the idea of nuking away a few million people." The presumption apparently is that one ought to be able to handle that idea, when in any sort of sane discourse the concept itself should be seen to be nothing less than monstrous.

How did we get to the point where we as a society can contemplate that sort of action and view it as normal or necessary? Were we always that way as a nation? I don't believe we were, but I believe we have experienced a hardening of the heart, an erosion of our moral sensitivity over the last generation begin-ning with World War II. A few examples might illustrate what I mean.

In the 1930s we viewed with horror the Krupp arms industry in Germany. We called these purveyors of lethal weapons to small nations "merchants of death" and condemned such arms traffic as unworthy of a civilized people. Today our own nation outstrips anything Krupp ever imagined, and the arms industry is so deeply embedded in our national economy that, to an alarming degree, our welfare depends on somebody's warfare.

In 1940 we were justly horrified when the Nazis put into effect Clausewitz's theory of total war, in which civilian populations were treated as though they were enemy combatants, and subjected to indiscrimate bombing and shelling, to being used as hostages and as objects of terrorism and reprisal. But it wasn't long before we found ourselves playing by the same rules and justifying it, i.e., the fire bombing of Dresden, and the bombing of Hiroshima and Nagasaki.

Faced with Axis aggression our nation underwent speedy and radical economic and industrial transformation beginning in 1940, which took us from a peacetime economy to a wartime one. But we've not been able to reverse that process in the last forty years and we still find ourselves tooled up for war rather than for peace. A wartime economy may work for a while, but in the long run it is disastrous. Whatever the motivation, it necessarily diverts virtually all of the technological, industrial, and scientific resources away from activities that could alleviate national and international problems of hunger, energy shortages, and social well-being, and puts them all into the nonproductive business of stockpiling weapons. All of this of course is done in the name of preserving our peace and well-being. But it is more than legitimate to ask whether we may be causing ourselves more harm than that which we are seeking to avoid.

It is true that since 1945 at least no one has used nuclear weapons. This is often pointed to as a justification for the nuclear arms race. The sky has not fallen, we are told. The threat of "mutually assured destruction" (MAD) is the only effective deterrent. Only God knows if that is true. Certainly in human history, arms races have inevitably led to war. And while it may be true that the possession of large arsenals of nuclear weapons has kept an uneasy truce, the cost of human suffering appears high. The sky may not be falling, but the earth may be rotting. And we have become a culture capable of "handling the idea of nuking away a few million people."

In the face of such cosmic evil from which there appears to be no simple escape, the doctrine of Christian pacifism appears to be very attractive. But for me at least it also appears to be impossible. Violence so pervades our society that even if one refuses to participate in any active violence, there appears to be no escape from becoming an accomplice in violence by passive acquiescence when one's neighbor or one's family is attacked. But that brings me back to my principle thesis. The very causes which seem to make absolute pacifism impossible make active peacemaking obligatory.

Peacemaking, properly understood, is at the heart of the Gospel, and biblically it is the one activity through which the divine image is most clearly seen. "Blessed are the peacemakers for they shall be called the children of God."

If my time in Latin America showed me the demonic face of violence, my years of involvement in various renewal movements within the church have brought me into contact with the only possible solution to the problem, and have saved me from losing hope. The Gospel, I have come to see, offers the possibility of our participation in God's new creation, not simply a method for rearranging the broken pieces of the old one. There is a potential for true cosmic redemption through the power of God's spirit to make all things new. I have begun to see with greater clarity what Paul meant when he said, "We are not contending against flesh and blood but against the principalities, against the powers, against the rulers of this present darkness, against the spiritual hosts of wickedness in the heavenly places." (Ephesians 6:12)

The warfare is spiritual, and to spiritual conflict we must bring spiritual weapons. The "whole armor of God," which Paul describes, is an excellent agenda for active peacemakers, and I suspect that the more attention we pay to it, the more effective our efforts will be.

One of the essential elements is prayer. Unfortunately, prayer is often the last thing that many who work for peace think of. But peacemaking reflects the heart and the will of the Father and is not simply the activity of a few interested individuals. To be a peacemaker is to begin by praying for peace.

What can we expect God to do when we pray for peace? There was a time when I expected those prayers to be answered by the Lord's simply putting an end to the fighting, stopping the wars, and reducing the overall level of violence in our society. I assumed that I would be a spectator, watching the process from the sidelines. But that kind of picture belongs to a fantasy world, a make-believe universe.

The Hebrew word *shalom,* which we generally translate as "peace," is a far richer word than its English equivalent. It means much more than the absence of conflict. It means the presence of those just and equitable relationships between people, and between people and the Lord, which one might describe as a condition of total well-being for all. Or to put it another way, if peace means the absence of conflict, then it also means the elimination of all those factors that produce conflict and the establishment of the kind of just and equitable society where conflict in unnecessary. In shalom, our two initial concerns of peacemaking and feeding the hungry become almost synonymous.

To pray for peace means to pray for a rearrangement of some of the pieces of our own life, an alteration in our life-style and standard of living. It is to ask the Lord to take away some of our toys, particularly those which consume so much fossil-fuel energy. It is to ask the Lord to reduce our surplus in order that other people and nations might simply have enough. We cannot call that state of affairs peace where the starving are asked to keep quiet so as not to disturb the sleep of the overfed. To pray for peace means to pray for the removal of those malignancies which hinder the world's health.

Prayer and action belong together. Someone remarked that action without prayer is presumptuous, but prayer without action is blasphemous. How then can we act as peacemakers?

New Testament teaching and human experience agree that we should begin with the smaller things before tackling the larger ones. When asked for some life-changing advice by a journalist, Mother Teresa replied, "Smile at the people you live with!" We will try peacemaking with those we live and work with before attempting it on an international scale. And we might try to convert the Christian church before we try the Pentagon and the Kremlin.

I believe we must begin to convert attitudes and presuppositions before we can effectively challenge actions. Our attitudes toward violence as a remedy for anything must change. There is a warning explicit in the Christian message about individuals and nations who rely on violence and threats of violence to protect themselves. "Those who live by the sword will die by the sword." I believe the Lord is speaking here of our own sword, not someone else's. Our reliance on violent attitudes and behavior will harden our hearts and consume us in such a way that our true life will disappear.

Another attitude has to do with classical Christian definitions of "just wars." My own belief is that the term itself is a contradiction in terms. There may be times when war is seen to be the lesser of two evils, but it remains evil and cannot be called "just." But the concept of a just war becomes totally meaningless when we are faced with the prospect of nuclear war. No one can win a nuclear war. There is simply attack and retaliation — which destroy both participants and many others as well. There is no way in a nuclear conflict for destruction to be limited to active combatants, no way it can serve a just purpose. It is as insane as the concept of destroying a village in order to save it. There are some diseases for which the apparent cure is worse than the disease itself.

With changed attitudes may come some changes in direction. I hope that, together, Christians can encourage those in positions of political power to renounce all first-strike intentions, and then to work tirelessly for an end to the arms race, and a gradual reduction of all nuclear weapons until they disappear from the face of the earth.

This latter may sound utopian. Faced, however, with a choice between utopianism and suicide I would hope the Christian would opt for the former.

There is no way to tell whether any peacemaking efforts will be successful. But then we have never been told what the outcome of our obedience will be, we have simply been told to obey. Jesus said at one time, "when the Son of Man comes, will he find faith on earth?" In other words, will he find anybody faithfully obeying what he has told us to do by word and example? On a personal level I want to be found faithful. Regardless of the ultimate outcome of my efforts I want to be a peacemaker so that whatever happens first, the Lord's coming or my going, I'm found faithfully engaged in those things which make for peace. How tragic it would be for the Prince of Peace to discover that he has no followers.

PETITIONING GOD FOR PEACE
Glen Stassen

We were only a small group of people of faith in Louisville, Kentucky — not

Glen Stassen is an associate professor of Christian ethics at the Southern Baptist Seminary in Louisville. He is also deacon in the Crescent Hill Baptist Church, and on the board of the local Council on Peacemaking and Religion.

exactly the center of national power. And for some of us, at least, it was becoming a problem of faith: Is God really Lord of history, or are the forces of nuclear madness in control?

We were becoming increasingly aware of dangerous and powerful forces moving us toward a nuclear war that would end the lives of those we love. We were experiencing some fear, despair, and frustration because we seemed unable to divert those forces. Was there some way we could participate in God's activity so that we would not simply be waging a lonely and losing battle against the principalities and powers?

And so we were driven, not by clever strategizing, but by our own need for faith, to meet together to pray.

It was the Sunday evening before Hiroshima Day, 1978, at a downtown Presbyterian church, when we first met to pray for peace. We invited respected representatives from various denominations who shared a concern for peacemaking to lead our prayers and meditations.

The service had been announced in church bulletins and during congregational services. But primarily we relied on personal invitations: We got busy asking individual members of our congregations to come and offered to give them rides. Not only did a large number of people come, but we were given an indication of interest and need that resulted in a sense of shared community with fellow church members from all over Louisville. The service had an impact on the on-going life of all our congregations. Ever since then, prayer for peace has been a likely occurrence in regular Sunday morning worship services around town.

After our first joint service we served refreshments and stayed around to talk. This, too, we have come to do regularly. We believe people feel lonely in opposing the nuclear threat, and we believe sharing in community is central to biblical faith. As we talked, the excitement and sense of release and hope that people were expressing made it clear that praying for peace together had met a deep need and had been profoundly meaningful.

We learned that many people have fears about nuclear war that are seldom or never confessed in formal worship. Consequently, they experience an internal split between a formal worship that does not make contact with their deep concern and a life full of concern that is not honestly confessed before God and community. To fuse the two together, to confess the anxiety in prayer before God, and to experience community with others expressing similar fears can be a moving experience that breaks one out of tightly held bonds and joins one to others with new wholeness and integrity.

And so it should not be surprising that we did it again; and that we felt a sense of affirmation when we began two years ago to join in calling for annual prayer services for peace on Memorial Day weekend and later learned that one hundred fifty congregations and communities across the nation had met to pray in response.

Two years ago we held our prayer service on Monday evening at Crescent Hill Baptist Church; it was a beautiful evening, and we met outdoors on the wide front steps extending upward toward the sanctuary. We were facing north, the direction from which the nuclear missiles will come, if and when they come. We were facing the threat we usually prefer to repress. The prophets and Jesus often warned of the threat of war, and we believe honest hope cannot come unless we face the threat.

We prayed, on Memorial Day, that there would not be another war to give more dead to be memorialized. We prayed for victims of past and present wars, not only in this country but in others: Ireland, Iran, Afghanistan, Zimbabwe, Palestine, Israel. And we prayed for the future victims of nuclear war in the United States and the Soviet Union and elsewhere around the world.

As we prayed and listened to meditations on the front steps of the church that quiet Memorial Day evening, there were occasional passersby on foot and in cars. Apparently they were surprised to see us — you could see it on their faces — many waved, smiled, and honked a brief hello. Our worship turned into celebration and a sense of community with one another and with the passersby. The free feeling of moving from the sanctuary to the outdoors, the sense of moving from private prayer to open confession in communal worship, the opportunity to participate in witness to passersby, the beautiful May evening, the fresh air, all combined to give us a sense of celebration and participation in God's creative and redemptive action.

We wanted to help other congregations share in the experience of praying for peace, not just when we came together from many churches, but within their own congregations. Many have severed the connection between Christian worship and peacemaking. So last year we worked together with several pastors representing the major denominations and the Jewish Temple to form a Council on Peacemaking and Religion. (For information on the council's work, write to it at 3940 Poplar Level Road, Louisville, KY 40213.) At its first meeting the council succeeded in persuading six churches to hold their own Memorial Day prayer services for peace. We found it much easier to reach out to new congregations if we worked through their pastors. The pastors suggested that we would reach more people if such services were held on Sunday at a time when people were used to attending worship, and if they were held indoors.

We approached other pastors about holding a prayer service on the Sunday before Hiroshima Day and Nagasaki Day (August 6 and 9), and on a Sunday during Advent. Then we encouraged them to make prayers for peace a part of their regular worship services during the year. We suggested that they might consider forming a World Peacemaker group with our help. These groups are an idea of Church of the Saviour. (The church will send a peacemaker manual; the address is 2852 Ontario Road NW, Washington, DC 20009.) We also offered to help them undertake their own study of peacemaking issues, which could lead them to form an ongoing group.

In our own Memorial Day weekend prayer services we often invite people from various nations to lead prayers, as well as people who represent various age and interest groups. In one service, a South Korean Christian, an African seminary student, an Indian, and a Japanese, all from nations where the impact of war are real, led us in prayers for peace. A member of the church youth group who symbolizes our caring for the future of our youth, a leader of the

Woman's Missionary Union who represents our concern for other nations, and a middle-aged veteran who bears in his own person the memory of wars we are memorializing, each led us in prayer. We want to heal potential differences of viewpoint and group loyalty by bringing together persons of faith from different groups in the church.

At the same time, we have sought people not only for their representativeness, but also for their sincere faith. In our service last year the most moving prayer was offered by the veteran, who remembers the agony of war and who prayed profoundly about the roots of war, confessing how they reach down into our own selfhood, asking that we dig them out so war might not do its awful damage once again.

We usually include time as well for silent prayer and for spontaneous prayer. Openness to the Spirit to speak in different ways through different people is important if we are to pray deeply and urgently.

We pray about the causes of war, and about our relation to those causes. We utter our own fears and anxieties, we pray for our children and others we love and for children and loved ones in other countries. Mostly we pray prayers of confession and repentance; we find that until we can confess our deep, usually repressed concerns, admonitions to action feel superficial and burdensome. But when we do come together in deep and real prayer, there is a sense of release and an experience of new wholeness from which more centered action can flow.

On some occasions we have invited the newspapers and television, and have been given dramatically extensive coverage, especially when we prayed on Sunday afternoon in the Catholic cathedral downtown. Ironically, we made much more news praying, when we were not looking to make news, than we did when some of us paraded together in picturesque fashion before the Federal Building, or dramatized the story of the nuclear arms race at the Belvedere, Louisville's public plaza.

Our services do move toward celebration. We celebrate our sense of community with one another in prayer. We celebrate the presence of God, who does not will the awful destruction of nuclear war, who suffers with those who suffer, and who allows us to participate in his redemptive action.

In the Memorial Day Service at Christ Church Cathedral in Louisville, people wrote their prayers on pieces of paper and fastened them to helium-filled balloons. The releasing of the balloons was an expression of hope, as well as a symbolic joining with other nations toward which the winds were blowing. And while the balloons were beginning their flight, members celebrated their community with one another by sharing in strawberry ice cream and warm fellowship.

This year we have sent letters to ninety-seven congregations, suggesting that they have their own prayer services on Memorial Day weekend, and offering to help them plan services and find speakers. Again, the principle of personal invitation is the key: We are organizing pastors and people from each denomination to follow up the letters with phone calls urging other pastors to hold services.

We'd like to issue an invitation to non-Louisvillians to pray with us on Memorial Day weekend in your own congregations or communities.

Appendix B:

The Arms Race in the News

THE MYTH OF POWER, THE POWER OF MYTH
Richard J. Barnet
Reprinted from *Christianity and Crisis,* 27 November 1978.

"If we can't get disarmament out of a group like this, I'm afraid we're just not going to get it." The time was April 1961, a day or two before the Bay of Pigs. The place was the State Department auditorium. The speaker was John J. McCloy, then just appointed by President Kennedy as his adviser on disarmament. The "group like this" was the cream of the country's missile makers, Pentagon planners, and warrior intellectuals who had gathered to discuss the challenge of disarmament. It was my first day at official work in the disarmament business, and my introduction into the theater of the absurd.

Now, seventeen years later, a general — he may have been in the audience that day for all I know — is named the new head of the U.S. Arms Control and Disarmament Agency to convey the same obvious message: There isn't going to be any disarmament.

Most people have no trouble believing that message. The world arms budget is now $400 billion a year. The United States is planning to spend something like $1.8 trillion in the next ten years on the military. Both the United States and Soviet Union are poised on the threshold of new and incredibly dangerous weapons systems — highly accurate warheads, intricate gear for fighting computer-programmed limited nuclear wars, new and more powerful intercontinental missiles, lasers, killer satellites, and other "war-winning technology" — all of which will make the military environment much less stable than it is today. Military planners on both sides experience increasing pressures to keep nuclear strike forces on increased alert, to move toward "launch on warning" strategies so as to protect increasingly vulnerable missiles and to strive for a "technological breakthrough" to disarm the enemy. These pressures are making the world a much more dangerous place than it has been at any time since the dawn of the nuclear age.

For the first twenty years of the nuclear era the arms race was one-sided; the Soviets matched the U.S. arsenal with Khrushchevian threats rather than missiles and bombs. Now we see a world in which both sides have remarkably similar forces, similar bureaucracies for rationalizing and managing those forces, and similar doctrines governing their use. Ironically, in the years of the negotiations for a Strategic Arms Limitation Treaty (SALT) these dangerous developments have accelerated. While the statesmen haggled over SALT I, the stockpile doubled and the technology raced ahead. When the haggling ended, not a single weapon had been destroyed.

The danger of nuclear war in the 1980s is awesome. The reason is not merely that inherently more dangerous weapons are being built but also that these weapons are becoming inevitably drawn into life-and-death struggles around the world. The cold war, we can now see in retrospect, was a relatively peaceful affair. Despite the cosmic ideological issues over which the United States and the Soviets occasionally threatened to blow up the world, there wasn't very much to fight about and the half-dozen men or so in Russia and America with a finger on the button never had any compelling reason to push it. The perceived need to avoid nuclear war was greater than either side's concern over the outcome of any particular encounter.

This is not necessarily so for other beleaguered political figures of our time. The rulers of South Africa, sworn to maintain the domination of fifteen million blacks by four million whites on a black continent, are obvious customers for the technology of nuclear mass terror. Whether they actually have the bomb or, as is perhaps more likely, are in a position to acquire it whenever they wish is a detail. The threat of a nuclear Masada in southern Africa is staring us in the face.

The list of potential flashpoints for nuclear war is a long one. Idi Amin or some other despot with a ravaged brain; terrorist groups, with or without a cause; sophisticated criminals engaged in private enterprise blackmail — all have plausible reasons to acquire, or to make the world believe they have acquired, nuclear weapons and the will to use them. And the materials and technology for creating nuclear weapons are ever more widely available.

These developments greatly increase the likelihood of new U.S.-Soviet confrontations. In future confrontations we cannot always count on the Soviets backing down; their remarkable record of restraint in a crisis (even those they provoke) is a reflection of their relative military weakness in the past. Having achieved rough parity with the United States in military power, their national security managers are now much more likely to think like their U.S. counterparts: "We can't afford to back down and be exposed as a pitiful, helpless giant." Thus the happy accident that the world has survived the first thirty-five years of nuclear era is unimpressive evidence that we can avoid nuclear war in the coming era, for world power relationships are changing faster than we can comprehend and the arms race has become an entirely new game. The impending new stage of the military competition is likely to make the world of the 1970s look in retrospect like a Quaker village.

Why then is there no rush to disarm?

The answer, it seems to me, must be sought on many levels. To begin with, it has been a long time since the purposes of disarmament or the expectations from disarmament were made clear. It is evident that in the present political climate "zero nuclear weapons" is merely a rhetorical goal, whether the rhetorician is the President of the United States or a spokesperson of the peace movement. With the spread of nuclear weapons and nuclear technology the call for physical abolition of all nuclear weapons without regard for the political, moral, and psychological changes that must accompany radical disarmament merely heightens anxiety and breeds cynicism.

Since we have long passed the point at which putting the weapons physically out of reach would make us much safer — to avoid an utterly catastrophic holocaust more than 95 percent of present stockpiles would have to be destroyed — most people have lost sight of what disarmament is supposed to achieve. Because we cannot visualize an alternative road to security except through stockpiling arms, we focus on the risks of disarmament rather than the advantages. Even the most minimal arms agreements involve the issue of transferring trust — from weapons we do not understand and cannot see but believe in — to shadowy foreign leaders whom we have been taught to distrust. Since the purposes of disarmament are unclear and the implications uncertain, most people prefer to stay with the world we know or think we know than enter a world in which we put our trust in the sanity and decency of people rather than the power of machines.

There has been no disarmament because the assumptions of the arms race have been almost universally accepted. Most people, including most people who favor disarmament, accept the premise that more weapons mean more security, that alternative systems of security not based on making hostages of hundreds of millions of people are utopian, and that the survival of the United States as a sovereign actor in the world justifies mass murder, poisoning of the earth, and the hideous mutation of the human species.

We do not seem to be able to generate the moral passion to rid the world of arms because we ourselves are psychologically dependent upon them. The role of nuclear terrorism in our society is parallel to that of slavery a little over a hundred years ago. Like slavery, nuclear terrorism is a monstrous evil that mocks both our religious pretensions and our virtues. Both are dehumanizing. Both make victims of the innocent. Both are justified by worshiping power. Both support the comforts of the well-off and the aspiring. Both systems are addictive social drugs with a hold over society that cannot be broken except by the expression of extraordinary moral passion, courage, and the will to break free. The moderate use of nuclear weapons, like the moderate use of slavery, is impossible for the same reason the Missouri Compromise failed. Systems have their own dynamics. Arms control — banning certain weapons while building others more efficient and more terrible — cannot succeed because it perpetuates, rather than challenges, the system of nuclear terrorism.

To say you are for disarmament means — unless you are indulging in official rhetoric — that you renounce the war system. Disarmament is a way of conveying intentions and establishing social commitments that are completely inconsistent with the use of blackmail, terror, and brute force as instruments of national policy. Most of us are unwilling to reflect on how much we depend upon the war system for personal security and comfort. That was also true of slavery, and for that reason more than two hundred years intervened between the first pangs of Quaker conscience and the Emancipation Proclamation.

As with slavery, our economic dependence upon the war system is profound as well as anachronistic. Both once made short-term economic sense; but the war system, like slavery, has outlasted its time because it blocks possibilities for much more efficient and rational use of resources and more effective means of developing power to solve political and social problems.

Though the war economy has brought us inflation, technological backwardness, maldistribution of wealth, a sinking dollar, and unemployment, it is the economic drug we use to keep unemployment from becoming worse. (About 250,000 defense-related jobs were created in the recent recession through increases in the military budget.) The war economy provides comfortable niches for millions of bureaucrats in and out of military uniform who go to the office every day to build nuclear weapons or to plan nuclear war; millions of workers whose jobs depend upon the system of nuclear terrorism; scientists and engineers hired to look for that final "technological breakthrough" that can provide total security; contractors unwilling to give up easy profits; warrior intellectuals who sell threats and bless wars.

Undergirding the military-industrial complex is a series of myths about security.* Real progress toward disarmament means confronting these myths on two levels. On the first level we need to demystify the arcane world of national security analysis by focusing on it the withering light of common sense. The nuclear liturgy of the Pentagon, its acolytes in the Congress, and its captive think tanks is conducted in a dead language for familiar reasons: It protects the priesthood from troublesome questions. At a deeper level we cannot avoid probing the psychological and spiritual sickness within us which makes us so ready to accept the moral absurdity of nuclear war.

Puncturing the myths at the level of logic is not difficult. But it is rarely done. The disarmament advocates are drawn into the debate on terms set by the warrior institutions; we find ourselves pontificating about yields, throw-weights, and relative vulnerabilities. Or we launch crusades against individual weapons systems — the B-1 for example — which disppear like the Cheshire Cat only to reemerge with a new name in some more expensive form. Yet the Pentagon's greatest point of vulnerability lies elsewhere. What the guardians of the war system are able to conceal from us when we debate on their terms is the Pentagon's inability to deliver its products: defense and deterrence.

As in a shell game, we are deceived by being distracted. They began deceiving us the moment they changed the name of the War Department to the Department of Defense. The Pentagon is still quite capable of making *war*, but several years ago it lost the ability to provide the nation with any effective *defense*. The National Security Council recently revealed the results of its study "PRM-10," which concluded that in a nuclear war with the Soviet Union 140 million Americans would probably be killed. (More than 100 million Soviet citizens would die too.) Yet we are unable to make the intellectual leap required by the technology of contemporary warfare.

*See President Eisenhower's farewell address on page 43.

There *is* no defense, if we are scrupulous enough to observe the ordinary meaning of the word. According to *Webster's New International Dictionary,* defense means "protection" or "warding off an attack." The Soviet Union has about 4,000 nuclear weapons capable of being dropped on or hurled at the territory of the United States, 150 of them on submarines just off our territorial waters. (That the U.S. maintains more efficient submarines with some 3,000 nuclear weapons just off the Soviet coast does not make the United States any more defensible.) One hundred nuclear weapons falling on the United States or the Soviet Union, a Secretary of Defense stated more than four years ago, would kill more than thirty-five million people and destroy almost two-thirds of the industrial capacity of either nation.

In 1969 the United States and the Soviet Union concluded, after each had spent billions on research and development, that an effective antiballistic missile system could not be built. Fallout shelters might increase the number of survivors of a nuclear attack and swell the population fated to die a lingering death from radiation, but "civil defense" is a complete misnomer. The population cannot be protected. When we spend the next $1.8 trillion and they match it, as of course they will, we will be no closer to defense than we are now.

The second product is deterrence, and that also is mostly sleight-of-hand. The standard nightmare that we are supposedly deterring is a Soviet attack or Soviet blackmail. If we fall short of the magic number of nuclear weapons, it is argued, Kremlin leaders may think that they would suffer *only* 10 million or 20 million or 50 million casualties if they push the button; they may then conclude that running the world with the United States out of the way would be worth it.

There is nothing in Soviet behavior, history, or ideology to suggest that the model of the Soviet leader waiting by the button until the computer predicts an "acceptable" casualty level is anything but a convenient Pentagon fantasy to support an unending arms race. It is said that it is a harmless fantasy, a kind of insurance policy against Armageddon. But, unlike an insurance policy, the arms race directly affects the risk. By preparing for an implausible war we make other scenarios for nuclear wars — wars by accident and miscalculation — far more probable.

Anyone who ponders the elaborate system of war prevention we have erected — people in submarines submerged for months waiting for the word to destroy four hundred cities with the touch of a button, banks of computers that are expected to behave significantly better in communicating critical information than those that produce the billing foul-ups in department stores, cool rational leaders whom we expect to make the most agonizing decisions in a crisis, without information, without sleep — will not have difficulty agreeing with the growing number of scientists who state flatly that nuclear war is now inevitable.

But logic pitted against fantasy does not convince, and the power of the war system is rooted in fantasy. Until we can increase the level of self-awareness to enable us to confront those myths of terror and power that swirl in our collective subconscious, the peace movement can win all the debates and lose everything. Most people who think about the question at all accept the proposition that if you want peace, you must prepare for war. The whole debate about nuclear strategy is really a debate about human nature — whether the will to domination in people can be displaced by the building of a just society, or must be restrained by superior force. Most of us believe the latter, and there is impressive historical evidence to support that belief. (There is also impressive historical evidence that the effort to restrain putative aggressors inevitably produces arms races and that these generally end in war.)

The modern nation-state, which for most of us defines our reality, was built on the war system. Never mind that even before the nuclear era the magnification of war has destroyed even the victors — Britain lost its preeminence with its costly victory in World War I, and the sun set forever on the British Empire when it repeated the triumph thirty years later — most people still think of war and the threat of war as the road to security, national and personal.

There is a terrible irony that as the state has lost the power to defend its people, out of desperation they identify ever more closely with it. Not the government, which is blamed for everything, but the state as the symbol that gives meaning to individual lives. In a society without religion, without community, bereft of tradition, overwhelmed by massive change, the individual reaches for the flag as protective wrapping. The state becomes the instrument for the exercise of vicarious power, and war the instrument for venting personal frustration and hatreds.

We in the United States have not experienced war within our own borders since the time of Lincoln. With the exception of Korea and Vietnam, for most Americans war has been on the whole a rather pleasant experience, profitable for many, contributing greatly to national power and prestige. World War I certified our "great power" status; World War II made us "No. 1" and restored a sick economy. Meantime, the generation of Soviet citizens with direct experience of the suffering and loss of war is passing from the scene. People do understand that war is terrible, that nuclear war would multiply the horror; but their knowledge is abstract, historical, less compelling than other fears.

One reason there is renewed anti-Soviet feeling in the country is that it is easier now than it was a few years back to make a plausible case for a "Soviet threat," because the Soviets are trying to match and perhaps surpass the United States in certain weapons. But apart from the fear this can generate, apart from resentment of Soviet-Cuban involvement in Africa and dislike for Soviet repression of dissidents, there is deeper reason for anti-Soviet sentiment. Beset by fundamental change, this nation has political, economic, and institutional *need* for an enemy. The Russians fill the need because they symbolize the steady diffusion and realignment of global power now under way and our consequent growing inability to control political events in the world.

That is an unsettling reality that not only saps our sense of national power but reaches into our personal lives. During the war in Vietnam many Americans, who did not know where or what Indochina was, internalized official propaganda and talked passionately about the threat from the Vietnamese. So also now we use the Russians as metaphors for other fears: anxiety about loss of property, loss of job, loss of status, and fear for personal safety in a city or for an impoverished old age. The Soviets are responsible for none of these, and they would not disappear if the Soviet land mass melted or the Czar returned to the Winter Palace. Seen in realistic perspective, the USSR is a conservative opportunistic power with uncertain ambitions that we can be sure will behave ever more adventurously in an atmosphere of growing military competition.

Because fear feeds on itself, military rivalries tend by their nature to intensify until the explosion comes. Accommodations between fearful rivals are not impossible; less than five years before he went to Peking to make a quasi-alliance with the Chinese, Brzezinski was warning that they were a great threat to our national security. But in the climate of opinion our competition with the powerful Soviet Union creates, it is difficult to imagine other modes of coexistence, better means of achieving security.

At the dawn of the nuclear age Albert Einstein said that everything had changed but our thinking. When he said that politics was more difficult than physics he was emphasizing the extraordinary resistance we have to insights that could bring peace. Because thinking must fundamentally change if there is to be disarmament, and because fundamental change appears nearly impossible, the task of disarmament or ending the war system is more formidable than that of any social movement in history.

Recognizing this is necessary if we are to gather strength for the struggle. The peace movement has so little support, public opinion polls confirm, because of widespread feelings of powerlessness and universal mechanisms of denial. We feel powerless to alter the course of events, and so we deny both the danger and our responsibility to confront it.

But we will compound our feelings of powerlessness if we impose unreal expectations on ourselves. Many of us assume that once the facts are presented and the moral issues raised militaristic forces will disperse, so that we lose heart when they are not exorcised by a pamphlet or a march or a prayer. I believe that we need to see ourselves as part of a historic process, like the successive generations of abolitionists, to confront the institutions of war relentlessly and passionately, to build on the achievements of the peacemakers of the past, to honor our own achievements, such as the ending of the Vietnam war, and to keep alive the faith that decency and rationality can prevail. Greater realism about the extraordinary obstacles to a security system based on disarmament can be inspiring rather than dispiriting because we can better understand both ourselves and the nature of the task.

A new security system for humankind is inevitable. The only question is whether it will come before nuclear war or after. More than any other issue, peace can command overwhelming majoritarian support. But disarmament, which is a mechanical technique for achieving peace, is not such an issue standing by itself. Zero nuclear weapons will be a reality on the day some clerk finds the last forgotten weapons in some abandóned warehouse and calls the department of waste disposal to get rid of them. To devalue them we need to delegitimize them, to keep stressing that whether or not they are exploded in anger, they cannot be used as instruments of power or as the foundation of security without destroying our society in the process.

Finally, the devaluing of nuclear weapons is directly dependent upon enhancing the value of life in the twentieth century. Whether we have the will to create a peaceful world depends upon how much human beings really value survival. If nuclear war comes, it will be because we have allowed our leaders to give up on the crushing problems of the century, because in some sense we have lost our collective will to live. The passion to sustain a new abolitionist movement can flow only from a positive vision of a just and caring society.

THE OUTLOOK FOR WORLD PEACE AND PROSPERITY
Jerry Richardson
Reprinted from *The Futurist,* December 1978.

The political map of the world has changed constantly through history. Nations have formed, developed, expanded, fought wars, and sometimes disappeared completely.

In the twentieth century, political change has reached breakneck speed: monarchy has declined, the communist states have risen, and Western-style democracy has moved toward cradle-to-grave welfare. Colonial empires have disintegrated and dozens of new nations have appeared; in fact, the number of independent countries doubled between 1945 and 1976. During that same thirty-year period, world population increased by 1.7 billion, passing the 4-billion mark in 1976. The gross world product (GWP) has been soaring, too. Between 1950 and 1970, the GWP climbed from $700 billion to $3.2 trillion (current prices).

With the formation of the League of Nations and its successor, the United Nations, the peoples of the world took the first hesitant steps toward world government. Thanks to modern transportation and communication breakthroughs, contact between nations now is at an unprecedentedly high level. International tourism is a booming industry, and international meetings of government officials and businessmen now are so commonplace that they rarely attract much attention.

But increased dialogue has not yet ended war as a means of settling differences. Millions of people died in World War I, tens of millions were killed during World War II, and hundreds of millions are likely to die if a third world war ever takes place. Furthermore, the proliferation of nuclear weapons of mass destruction, and the relative ease with which terrorist groups could gain access to these weapons have increased the danger of another major war.

Despite the great increase in the world's wealth, an immense disparity exists between the rich nations and the poor nations — a disparity that is a major source of concern to the world community. At the same time, leaders in both the rich and the poor countries are increasingly aware of the high level of interdependence that exists among today's societies. The developed countries depend on the underdeveloped countries for petroleum and other important natural resources. The poor countries, in turn, need the technological know-how and financial resources of the rich countries to improve their lot in the world.

This interdependence even extends to powerful rivals such as the United States and the Soviet Union. The Russians have relied heavily on the United States for grain in years past — so much so that some Kansas wheat farmers only half-jokingly referred to their state as "the breadbasket of the Soviet Union." On the other hand, the USSR has huge unexploited oil and gas reserves which one day may flow from Siberia across the Bering Strait and be carried by the Alaska pipeline to the continental United States and Canada.

Many international affairs experts think that the best hope for world peace lies in the recognition and development of an intricate network of interdependencies that will make it in the best interest of all nations to work together for their mutual benefit.

Among the important world problems to be dealt with in the years ahead are energy, mineral resources, food, population, environmental degradation, nuclear proliferation, the future of the United Nations, and the threat of global depression.

Total world military spending now stands at about $400 billion a year — more than $750,000 per minute. The U.S. Arms Control and Disarmament Agency estimates that the world spends more than two and a half times more money for military purposes than it does for public health. Furthermore, world military spending has doubled since the 1950s, even taking inflation into account. And there is no end in sight.

Although the United States, the Soviet Union, and their NATO and Warsaw Pact allies still account for about 70 percent of this total, a disturbing trend in recent years has been the sharp rise in military spending by Third World countries. More specifically, military spending in the Middle East, at constant prices, has quadrupled during the past seven years. Military spending in Africa rose from $1.4 billion dollars in 1967 to $5.9 billion in 1976. Seventy-five percent of the current world trade in major arms is with the Third World, reports the Stockholm International Peace Research Institute (SIPRI) in its 1978 *World Armaments and Disarmament Yearbook*. Ultimately, warms SIPRI, "the worldwide spread of weapons by the international arms trade may be as dangerous to world security as the U.S.-Soviet arms race and the spread of the capability to produce nuclear weapons."

But this does not mean that the latest developments on the nuclear weapons front are nothing to worry about. The tens of thousands of nuclear weapons in the arsenals of the world today are equivalent to one million Hiroshima-type atomic bombs — enough destructive power to level most of the cities of the northern hemisphere, to kill the bulk of their inhabitants instantly, and to cause the deaths of millions more through radiation poisoning. And nuclear weapons technology grows more and more sophisticated. Both the United States and the USSR have increased the accuracy of their strategic nuclear warheads and have developed mobile intercontinental ballistic missiles.

The development of the cruise missile and the possible deployment of the neutron bomb could further fan the fires of nuclear proliferation, SIPRI's experts believe. The neutron bomb, an enhance-radiation reduced-blast nuclear weapon, is designed to kill people more efficiently while causing less damage to buildings. Critics fear that these "safer" bombs will make the use of nuclear weapons more likely, a perception which could cause more countries to want to acquire them. The cruise missile could increase nuclear proliferation because many countries may see it as a cheap alternative to the production of combat aircraft or the replacement of other weapons that become obsolete. "Most industrialized countries and some Third World ones are technically capable of producing cruise missiles indigenously," the SIPRI *Yearbook* reports. "Thus, their proliferation may prove to be among the most far-reaching military technological developments ever."

Six nations now have tested nuclear weapons — the United States, the USSR, Britain, France, China, and India. Israel is widely assumed to have nuclear bombs. The spread of nuclear technology for the generation of electricity makes it conceivable that as many as forty countries could have the capacity to produce nuclear weapons by the year 2000. By 1985, eleven countries that do not now have nuclear weapons will have plants for separating plutonium or enriching uranium in quantities large enough to make several bombs, according to Albert Wohlstetter (*Foreign Policy,* Winter 1977). Those countries are West Germany, Belgium, South Africa, Japan, Italy, Argentina, Taiwan, Pakistan, South Korea, Brazil, and Iran. Among the other countries that could possibly have nuclear weapons by the year 2000 are Austria, Mexico, the Netherlands, the Philippines, Spain, Sweden, Switzerland, Yugoslavia, Egypt, North Korea, and Libya. The possibility also exists that some of these countries, once they have nuclear bombs, will supply them to other countries or even to terrorist groups.

Richard K. Betts of the Brookings Institution has identified three categories of countries that he considers prime candidates for developing or acquiring nuclear weapons. "Pygmy" states such as Pakistan and Taiwan could use them to fend off much larger enemies (India and China). "Paranoid" states such as North Korea and South Korea might feel compelled to maximize their military capabilities in any way possible. "Pariah" states such as Israel, South Africa, and Taiwan — which are threatened by fanatical opponents and increasingly isolated from the rest of the world — perhaps have the strongest motivation to turn to nuclear weapons, says Betts (*Foreign Policy,* Spring 1977): "Pariahs have the clearest incentives to increase their military power, the least technical distance to go to build a bomb, and the least to lose in doing so." These three pariah countries have already been drawn closer together by their desperate plight and may even form a consortium pooling their nuclear capabilities to produce bombs, Betts suggests.

Another alarming trend is the increasing military use of outer space. SIPRI estimates that about 75 percent of all satellites launched have military uses. The Soviet Union allegedly has tested "hunter-killer" satellites that can be used to destroy other satellites, and the United States is working on a similar weapon. SIPRI, in its book *Outer Space — Battlefield of the Future?*, estimates that new outer-space weapons such as laser-beam and charged-particle-beam devices may be only a decade or so away. By that time, the space shuttle will be available for placing them into orbit. One positive aspect of the use of space for military purposes, however, is that satellites can be used to verify arms control agreements and to monitor the conflict areas of the world.

Sophisticated new weapons systems are constantly appearing in the arsenals of the industrialized countries, but in recent years the speed with which these new weapons are distributed to other countries has increased sharply. Twenty years ago, most of the weapons supplied to Third World nations were second-hand; today, the buyer nations demand and usually get sophisticated modern weapons, along with spare parts and training.

If the current rate of increase in military expenditure continues, the world will be spending about $1 trillion on arms in the year 2000. The current figure of about $400 billion is almost double the gross domestic product of the entire continent of Africa and is about twenty times the total official development assistance given by the developed countries to the undeveloped countries. Although there is no guarantee that an end to the arms race would bring an immediate increase in nonmilitary assistance to the world's poor countries, it is considered highly unlikely that such aid will increase very much unless the military budgets of the developed countries are reduced. Thus, the arms race is closely related to other international problems such as hunger, population growth, and economic development . . .

Nuclear proliferation is another problem that cannot be solved without international agreements — as long as even one country is willing to give other countries access to technology and raw materials that could be used to make nuclear bombs, the world will not be rid of nuclear proliferation. International cooperation is also emphasized as a key to keeping the global economy healthy, narrowing the gap between the rich and poor countries, producing enough food for all of the world's people, and reducing population growth in countries that cannot afford it.

Most of the world's countries now seem to be increasingly aware of the concept of global interdependence and willing to take at least some joint steps aimed at controlling pollution, slowing population growth, and stabilizing the prices of commodities such as tin, wheat, coffee, rubber, copper, and sugar.

The forum for most of these efforts at increased international cooperation has been the United Nations. For example, technical discussions have been taking place in UNCTAD (United Nations Conference on Trade and Development) on market conditions for eighteen commodities, and these discussions are expected to lead to some major international price stabilization agreements in the near future. Last year, thirteen Mediterranean countries and the European Economic Community (EEC) reached agreement on the principles of a treaty to control the discharge of industrial waste, municipal sewage, and agricultural chemicals into their coastal waters; the negotiations were carried out at a meeting sponsored by the United Nations Environment Programme (UNEP). Rafael Sales, Executive Director of the United Nations Fund for Population

Activities (UNFPA), says that almost all of the member countries of the United Nations now participate as either donors or recipients of population control assistance.

The United Nations, however, remains on the whole a very weak sort of international organization, and increasing numbers of people throughout the world are becoming convinced of the need for a true world government as the next logical step in the evolution of human civilization.

The achievement of such a world governing body through peaceful means in the near future appears highly unlikely, though. In fact, the future of the United Nations itself is threatened by the proliferation of newly independent countries since World War II. Countries with populations under five million now are in the majority in the United Nations General Assembly, notes political scientist Elmer Plischke of the University of Maryland, and the result has increasingly been the "tyranny of the majority." These tiny countries, which have the same voting power as the United States or China, pay only a minute amount of the UN's operating costs, says Plischke, and the disparity could be even greater in the future: "If the rush to independence and admission to the United Nations continues, and fifty potential states are added to the roster, then approximately one hundred fifty members — the principal beneficiaries of its programs — which jointly would pay only 3.5 percent of its costs, would exercise three-fourths of the voting power in determining those very multimillion-dollar programs. Despite United States objections, in several cases minimum contributors have already decided the outcome of important votes, including financial issues. The same problem of disparity exists in other global and regional agencies — and will intensify as proliferation continues."

Plischke suggests a number of ways this financial/voting imbalance could be ameliorated: Voting rights could be restricted to those countries that pay more than one-tenth of one percent of its budget (which would disqualify two-thirds of current UN members); some form of weighted voting could be introduced; or perhaps the major powers will eventually withdraw from the UN.

This controversy illustrates vividly the difficulty of achieving a viable form of world government. Some nations will demand "one country, one vote," while others will insist on "one dollar, one vote." Nationalism is very strong, and still intensifying in many parts of the world. The loyalties of peoples probably can be shifted from the national to the world lever, concludes Roger Hilsman in his book *The Crouching Future,* but "it might well take one or more wars of frightening proportions to establish a world state, and once established, mankind might well be destined to go through a series of violent civil wars as well."

Bruce C. Murray identifies three types of world government that could develop in his book *Navigating the Future:* (1) an imperial government consisting of "diverse peoples governed by a strong, centralized world government"; (2) a superstate, consisting of "homogeneous people living under a distributed authoritarian bureaucracy of the advanced nations"; and (3) a world confederation, consisting of "diverse peoples existing in largely autonomous regional 'states.' " Murray expresses hope that the United Nations will continue to survive and be part of an evolving world confederation, the alternative world government system that he believes "might emerge as the least unsatisfactory means of governing a world racked by widespread social dissatisfaction and by ecological problems of unprecedented magnitude."

Despite the almost universal belief that world government will be nothing more than a dream for many years to come, there is reason for hope for the future. Nations are beginning to cooperate with one another in a variety of organizations, both formal and informal. More than thirty years have passed since the atomic bomb was perfected — and civilization has not been destroyed. If mankind can muddle through until the perfection of solar power and/or nuclear fusion gives the world a virtually unlimited supply of energy and until an effective world government can evolve from the modest beginning already visible, the result could well be a supercivilization that will thrive for thousands of years.

U.S. ARMS BUILDUP RESHAPING ECONOMY
Guy Halverson
Reprinted from *The Christian Science Monitor,* 8 February 1980.

The Carter Administration's sudden move toward higher defense spending is leading to a fundamental reshaping of the giant U.S. economy.

Already, some economists and historians here are comparing the rearmament effort to the military buildup in the early 1940s and in the Korean War period. The long-term consequences, they say, are beginning to be clearly identified:

• The on-again, off-again recession now has probably been put on the back burner, thanks to new defense spending that could reach a whopping $230 billion annually by the mid-1980s.

At the least, any recession is expected to be sharply mitigated.

• The inflation rate will be exacerbated by government spending on thousands of new tanks, jet fighters, rockets, and helicopters, and on ammunition stockpiles and the other hardware of modern warfare.

• In the long run, many economists believe higher defense spending will lead to greater controls (including possible wage and price controls) over the entire civilian sector of the economy. The Pentagon, it is noted here, already is grousing about shortages of vital metals and other commodities and a lack of skilled manpower. It is looking at the private sector to fill these needs, possibly at the expense of consumer goods.

• Money for the new defense spending, moreover, is expected to come out of the civilian sector of the overall economy. The reason is that while federal expenditures for defense are rising, federal spending for social programs is not being sharply cut back. That, some economists argue, means that there will be less disposable income for Americans to spend on consumer goods.

• Hardest of all to gauge, perhaps, is what will happen to political attitudes. Historians and sociologists note that in the 1940s and 1950s — before the Vietnam war — the Pentagon (and the entire so-called "military-industrial complex") enjoyed widespread public clout.

Those in uniform basked in great prestige, and dissenters were largely ignored.

Could that happen again? Was the antiwar turbulence of the Vietnam period an anomaly? No one is yet sure.

The United States, argues Harvard University historian Frank Freidel, a leading expert on the New Deal and the 1930s, now is at a turning point.

"For ten years," he argues, "we've been aware of a major Soviet buildup, but hoped we were wrong."

Now, with the Soviet invasion of Afghanistan, we've "suddenly discovered" that the Soviets are willing to use their military muscle in ways we hadn't anticipated, he says.

The new defense buildup is going to "have a significant impact on the U.S. economy," argues Adm. Gene La Rocque (USN, ret.), director of the Washington-based Center for Defense Information. The center is a liberal "think tank" that has been critical of large-scale defense expenditures.

"We're on the threshold of a hugh military expansion," Admiral La Rocque argues. "Our treasury is broke. Every Monday morning, [the U.S. Treasury] has an auction to borrow money to get us through the week. Further, the federal deficit is not only large, but very large." Now defense spending, he argues, without any significant reduction elsewhere in the fiscal 1981 budget, will only accelerate the inflation rate.

Many economists would agree about the likely inflationary impact of stepped-up defense spending.

At the least, argues Dr. Beryl Sprinkel, vice-president and chief economist of the Harris Bank of Chicago, seeking to have "guns and butter at the same time," raises the possibility that the administration will put off adopting much-needed policies to "encourage greater capital formation" in the United States.

Franklin A. Lindsay, chairman of the research-policy group of the Committee for Economic Development (CED), urges that we must "avoid the error during the Vietnam buildup" of seeking to have both guns and butter that "created the overload which launched our now-chronic inflation."

If defense costs rise, argues Mr. Lindsay, chairman also of the New England-based Itek Corporation, "so must the revenues to pay for them."

In the 1950s, according to most economists, relatively high defense spending was offset by proportionately low levels of spending for social projects under the essentially conservative Eisenhower administration.

Under President Johnson, in the 1960s, the United States sought to have both "guns and butter."

But even the adverse effects of that policy were mitigated somewhat by the fact that the United States still had a "growing economy," notes Robert W. Hartman, a public finance specialist with the Brookings Institution. In that sense, there was some room for "guns and butter."

The economy of the 1980s is not a big-growth economy.

The clear "implication of the new Carter defense program," says Mr. Hartman, "although the administration has not yet said as much, is to add up to a squeeze on private consumption."

In turn, he notes, that may mean giving up tax cuts while keeping interest rates at relatively high levels.

"The important thing to remember is that in previous episodes [rearmament] we didn't start from such a high inflationary base," says George Hagedorn, vice-president and chief economist of the National Association of Manufacturers.

"In World War II, we actually started from a decade of deflation, of depression. Now we're starting from an inflation base of over 13 percent."

Dr. Friedel of Harvard, who is writing what many historians believe is the definitive biography of President Franklin Roosevelt (it is not yet completed, despite a number of volumes), also points out that in the late 1930s and early 1940s a large part of the nation was isolationist, making a military preparedness program more difficult. Today there is a strong "defense related" constituency.

Still, analysts here in part liken the rearmament efforts then, and more particularly in the 1940s and 1950s under Presidents Truman and Eisenhower, to what is happening now.

The reason for the similarity is that the military establishment already is discussing seriously the need for establishing greater control over scarce commodities and many power pools.

A number of defense programs, particularly involving aircraft, are facing production roadblocks because of lack of parts.

Titanium armor for aircraft, for example, takes from 90 to 100 weeks to be delivered. Forgings for aircraft frames require 114 weeks or so before delivery. Gold, silver, lead, and copper are all in scarce supply.

Manpower, particularly skilled workers, is also in short supply throughout industry. "There is today a shortage of skilled metal workers throughout the United States," argues James A. Gray, president of the National Machine Tool Builders Association.

A new study by this association finds that a hefty 70 percent of its member firms are reporting significant manpower shortages.

For that reason, many military officials are already known to be arguing within the administration for a more formal priority-system for materials and manpower — the effect of which would be to divert supplies away from consumer industries, such as commercial aircraft.

The essential components of such a detailed priority system are already in place, notes Gen. Henry A. Miley Jr. (USA, ret.), president of the American Defense Preparedness Association, which is comprised of individuals and defense-related firms.

Currently, the Pentagon has a twofold priority rating system — the so-called "DO" and "DX" system. Under the "DX" designation, a military project would have all-out priority over civilian material needs. But getting the administration to use the higher-priority DX designation on a more regular basis has been difficult since the President himself must authorize this higher designation.

Throughout the United States, there are at least 10,000 factories and plants that could be quickly hooked into such a comprehensive priority system. But would the public accept such a large-scale redirection of the civilian economy at this juncture?

Most officials here assume that conditions would have to get much worse abroad before that were to happen.

All the same, the feeling now is widespread that the course is set, for a while at least. Defense spending will rise. The military will fight harder to untangle production bottlenecks by tapping precious resources flowing to consumer-goods manufacturers.

And the American public will find itself in the middle of what promises to be a severe struggle for these resources.

WHY BUYING GUNS RAISES THE PRICE
OF OUR BUTTER

Lloyd J. Dumas
Reprinted from *Christianity and Crisis,* 27 November 1978

Both of the theories of aggregate economic behavior at present widely accepted in the United States lead to the expectation of a trade-off between the rates of inflation and unemployment. Keynesian macrotheory, on the one hand, focuses on the size of total demand (represented by government, business, and consumer spending) in relation to the size of full employment supply (the economy's maximum ability to produce goods and services). When total demand is too low, unemployment results, and the pressure toward inflation is minimal. When demand is too high, full employment is achieved, but the excess of spending generates inflation.

The Quantity Theory of Money, on the other hand, focuses on the size of the money supply. Assuming some degree of price flexibility, monetarist doctrine implies that money supply growth produces economic expansion. This new growth, of course, reduces unemployment, but it also increases inflationary pressure; shrinkage has the opposite effects.

Both theories share one problem. Over the past decade we have witnessed an unprecedented *simultaneous* occurrence of both high unemployment and high inflation. How is this to be explained?

To understand the situation one has to begin with the basic economic principle that money, in itself, has little inherent value. The real stuff of the economy is made up of productive resources (such as labor, machinery, land, factory buildings, etc.), the processes by which they are combined, and the goods and services that combination produces. What counts is the allocation of resources, the efficiency of their use and the way in which their produce is distributed among the population. Resource allocation and efficiency together determine the types, quantities, and qualities of goods produced. Money flows are thus only important to the extent that they are used, and what happens to the goods and services that are produced.

Since both major macrotheories direct primary attention to the size of economic aggregates alone (total demand and total supply in one case, total money stock in the other) and specifically away from the details of the composition of spending (what is purchased, how it is paid for, how it is used), they could not hope to capture the implications of that resource use for the functioning of the economy. Furthermore, they are focused on the short term, and so ignore long-term economic processes. Yet it is precisely in these fundamental questions of resource use and long-term effects that a major part of the explanation for the present high unemployment/high inflation situation lies.

What we have been experiencing in the economy of the 1970s is not the result of anything that has happened within that period alone. It is rather the surfacing of the effects of an extended process of cumulative deterioration of the U.S. economy. This decay is linked primarily and directly to the maintenance of persistently high military spending over the past third of a century. Rather than being a job-creating, income-stimulating boon to the economy, the arms race has been an enormous burden, destroying jobs, generating inflation, and generally sapping the nation's economic strength and security.

There are a number of major reasons why this is so. To begin with, military goods are peculiar in that they are neither consumption goods, contributing to the present standard of living (as are clothing, food, household cleaners, etc.), nor investment goods, increasing the economy's capacity to produce "standard of living" goods and services in the future (as are industrial machinery, factory facilities, and the like). In this sense, then, they are *economically* useless (which is not to say they do not have other usefulness). They do, however, use up labor, capital, and other productive resources and are not economically *costless*. Rather, they impose an "opportunity cost" on the economy, measured by the value of economicaɪɪy useful goods and services foregone which could have been produced with these resources.

Since the flow of money to military industrial firms and their work forces is not balanced by a production of goods and services that either those firms or their employees can buy, the potential for inflation exists as too much money chases after too few goods. Raising taxes enough to draw this excess money out of the economy could erase this pressure, but raising taxes apace with the expansion of the military budget has not been politically expedient, and so it has not generally been done. As a result, the inflationary pressure has made itself felt.

Yet another negative effect of military spending is related to the inefficiency generated by the ways in which military procurement has been carried out. On paper there are a considerable variety of incentive payment formulas designed into military contracts for the purpose of encouraging efficient production. In reality, because of various common procurement practices (not the least of which is ready contract renegotiation), all major military contracts are operationally "cost-plus" contracts.

The practice of paying actual production costs plus an amount for profit not only eliminates any pressure to hold costs down, but it encourages the purposeful expansion of costs as a method for maximizing the total inflow of revenues and hence enhancing the economic power and status of both the firm and its management. As cost-escalating managements, backed by the enormous purchasing power of their rich customer, the Department of Defense, bid in the marketplace for the productive resources they want, they drive up the price of those resources, a cost-push effect that feeds inflationary pressure throughout the rest of the economy.

But perhaps the single most important domestic economic effect of the arms race has been its impact on the rate of civilian technological progress in the United States. Technological progress is the straightforward result of taking people with appropriate training in engineering and the sciences, giving them the proper equipment and facilities with which to work, and setting them to searching for solutions to particular problems. To be sure, the new technical knowledge they find will not always be strongly conditioned by the kinds of problems they are addressing and the sorts of solutions they are seeking.

For the past several decades, a large fraction of the technology developing resources of this country — that is, something in the order of one-third to one-half of the nation's engineers and scientists — have been directing their attention full-time to military related research and development (R&D). That has been and is where the salaries are, where the grants are, where the prestige is. Predictably, the result has been an extraordinary increase in militarily relevant technological knowledge, side by side with a major retardation in the growth of civilian technology. The much-touted argument that there are major "spin-offs" from military research which nullify the negative effect of diverting technological resources away from civilian R&D is massively contradicted by straightforward empirical observation.

Decades of booming military R&D notwithstanding, the failure of U.S. civilian technological progress was so obvious and so widespread by the mid 1970s that it was clearly recognized by both the business and scientific establishment. Striking testimony of this recognition was given by the cover story of *Business Week* for July 3, 1978, entitled "Vanishing Innovation," and by the seventh annual report of the National Science Foundation, issued in 1976, describing the erosion of U.S. leadership in science and technology. The technological backwardness of basic U.S. industries such as steel, heavy machinery, shipbuilding, construction, railroads, etc. is no longer seriously disputed (though the reasons for this retardation are not widely agreed upon).

The key economic function of civilian technological progress lies in its contribution to the growth of productivity. Improved techniques and process contribute directly, increasing the amount of our output producible from a given amount of resources. Improvements in machinery design increase machine efficiency, while improvements in techniques of machine manufacture hold the prices of such equipment down, thereby encouraging their purchase by industry in general with consequent widespread gains in productivity. And it is the rise of productivity that allows raising costs of labor, materials, fuels, etc. to be offset and hence the cost per unit of product to be held down. If a 10 percent rise in the cost of labor is accompanied by a 10 percent increase in the amount of output producible by that same amount of labor, labor cost per unit remains unchanged.

As resources devoted to research and development in U.S. civilian technology declined, productivity improvement slowed accordingly, dropping off in the period 1965–75 to the lowest average rate among nearly all industrial countries. Because the cost-offsetting capacity of technological innovation had become seriously eroded, higher costs of labor, fuel, materials, etc. were increasingly passed along in the form of higher prices, producing a powerful inflationary effect.

And the dominoes kept tumbling. As prices rose higher, U.S. industry increasingly priced itself out of both foreign and domestic markets, resulting in cutbacks in domestic production, which in turn generated rising unemployment even in the face of high product demand. The very same mechanism that has generated inflation has also generated unemployment.

The growing noncompetitiveness of U.S. industry vis-a-vis foreign industry, the loss of our crucial civilian technological edge, did not happen overnight. It is the result of decades of diversion of key economic resources to nonproductive purposes resulting from our singleminded determination to pursue national security through military expansion. It will not be undone by anything so simplistic as a change in fiscal or monetary policy.

It has become a necessary condition for the economic revitalization of the United States to reach into the economy and purposefully redirect the nation's resources toward key civilian areas. Nothing short of this direct structural change will be capable of undoing the rotting of the nation's economic foundations that has been the legacy of decades of the arms race.

Yet it must be understood that accomplishing this shift of resources is no mean task. Setting aside for the moment any consideration of political or ideological obstacles, there is a real economic problem involved. The world of military-oriented research, development, design, and production operates differently from that of the civilian sector. Economic resources specialized to the former cannot be smoothly transferred to the latter without careful attention to the removal of impediments that this specialization has produced.

For example, the emphasis in military design is heavily on performance; little attention is paid either to the expense of the design process itself or, more importantly, to the implications of the design for the cost of manufacture. It is thus commonplace for engineers operating in the military sector in the United States to focus on a very narrow range of a field, so as to be expert in that small area. Platoons of engineers, each with differing expertise, are then used to design the total product. And these engineers are not required to be highly sensitive to cost considerations.

It will be no simple matter to move such specialists into civilian design, where cost of production is a critical consideration (since the product must be sold in a marketplace) and where squeezing out every last bit of performance is far less crucial. Changing their methods and mind-sets will require a carefully thought-out plan for retaining and reorientation.

Of course, the transition of engineers and scientists from military to civilian activity is only one aspect of the overall conversion problem. Nevertheless, it illustrates a common requirement of all components of the conversion process — the necessity for serious, detailed advanced planning. Ideally, such planning should be highly decentralized, simply because to be successful a conversion plan for a military facility, be it a base or an industrial establishment, must be tailored to the special characteristics of the facility and is best developed by those who know it best: the work force, management, and the community involved.

While it has become increasingly clear that reversal of the arms race is now an indispensable *economic* policy for returning the United States to a condition of constructive growth, it is of utmost *political* importance that concrete plans for assuring a smooth transfer of resources have been developed and are ready for implementation. This will serve two critical purposes. First, it will allay the fears of those working in the military sector that their personal economic security is threatened by those who would reverse the arms race (a crucial step toward broadening the political constituency for conversion). Second, it will unambiguously demonstrate that the formal U.S. commitment to negotiating arms limitation and disarmament treaties is real and strong. That of itself will be a contribution to national security and human survival.

LOOTING THE MEANS OF PRODUCTION
Seymour Melman
Reprinted from *The New York Times,* 26 July 1981.

"America in Ruins" is both the title and forecast of a 1981 report by the Council of State Planning Agencies, an organization of the planning and policy staffs of the nation's governors. The Council finds major deterioration in parts of the country's infrastructure — that is, vital services such as clean water, reliable transportation, efficient ports, and competent waste disposal, which are indispensable underpinnings for an industrial system. The reports finds — as any traveler on United States railroads knows — that "the maintenance of public facilities essential to national economic renewal has been deferred."

Simultaneously, the means of production of United States industry have been deteriorating.

Production incompetence, now endemic, is spreading fast, not only in the well-publicized case of automobile firms but also in the following industries: steel, machine tools, radio and television manufacturing, railroad equipment, precision optics, fine cameras, men's shoes, flatware, hi-fi electronics, etc., etc., etc.

As private and public managers become better at making money without making economically useful goods, a new issue finally will have to be confronted: Will American industry reach a condition of "no return," making the achievement of industrial renewal problematic?

The way that an economy uses its capital — its production resources — is a crucial determinant of its productivity and economic well-being.

By 1977, for every $100 of new (producers) fixed capital formation, the United States applied $46 to the military economy. In Japan, the ratio was $3.70 for the military. The concentration of Japan's capital on productive economic growth goes far to explain the current success of that country's industry, where productivity *grew* 6.2 percent in 1980. By contrast, with the United States' aging machinery stock, the average output per person in manufacturing industry *decreased* 0.5 percent in 1980.

The United States has "achieved" its present state of industrial deterioration by assigning to the military economy large quantities of machinery, tools, engineers, energy, raw materials, skilled labor, and managers — resources identified everywhere as the "fixed and working capital" that is vital for production.

Since a modern military budget is used to purchase such resources, it is, effectively, a capital fund. A large ratio of military to civilian capital formation drains the civilian economy. The viability of the United States as an industrial society is threatened by the concentration of capital in a fund that yields no product useful for consumption or for further production. This looting of the means of production on behalf of the military economy can only be accelerated as a consequence of the unprecedented size of the war budgets advocated by the Reagan Administration.

The vital resources that constitute a nation's capital fund cannot be enlarged by waving a budgetary wand. Neither can manufacturing facilities by multiplied by ever richer subsidies to the managers of military industry. Basic machinery, skilled labor, engineers, and scientists — all are finite in number and difficult to increase.

The concentration of capital on the military portends sharply diminished opportunity for a productive livelihood for most Americans. Clearly, a choice must be made as to where these resources will be used.

The accompanying list of trade-offs illustrates the kinds of choices that the Reagan Administration and the Congress are now making with their budget and tax plans, intended or not.

The following are principal sources of these data: military-program and unit costs, and cost changes (overruns), the Department of Defense: "SAR Program Acquisition Cost Summary (Unclassified)," Dec. 31, 1980, and related reports, and "Procurement Programs (P-1)," March 10, 1981; and news media reports. The civilian capital-cost data range from reported prices (machine tools, buses, trolleys) and reported Federal budget items to informed estimates of industrial-research and project costs and of costs of public works. Economic and engineering estimates are from Representative Les Aspin (Congressional Record, April 17, 1981); Prof. John E. Ullmann of Hofstra University; Mark Hipp, a Colum-

bia University doctoral candidate; the Council on Economic Priorities; the city
of San Diego; and the California Public Policy Center.

Seven percent of the mili- = $100 billion = the cost of rehabilitating the
tary outlays from fiscal United States' steel industry so
1981 to 1986. that it is again the most efficient in the world.

The cost overrun, to = $ 8.4 billion = the comprehensive research-
1981, on the Navy's and-development effort needed
Aegis-Cruiser program. to produce 80- to 100-mile-
per-gallon cars.

The cost overrun, to = $ 42 billion = for California, a 10-year invest-
1981, on the Navy's cur- ment to spur solar energy for
rent submarine, frigate, space, water-, and industrial-
and destroyer programs. process heating; this would involve 376,000 new jobs and lead
to vast fuel savings.

Sixty-three percent of the = $110 billion = the 20-year cost of solar devices
cost overruns, to 1981, on and energy-conservation equip-
50 current major wea- ment in commercial buildings,
pons systems. saving 3.7 million barrels of oil
per day.

The cruise-missile pro- =$ 11 billion = the cost of bringing the annual
grams. rate of investment in public
works to the 1965 level.

Two B-1 bombers. = $400 million = the cost of rebuilding
Cleveland's water-supply
system.

Cost overruns, to 1981 on = $ 33 billion = the cost of rehabilitating or
the Navy's Trident and reconstructing one out of five
the Air Force's F-16 pro- United States bridges.
grams.

The Navy's F-18 fighter = $ 34 billion = the cost of modernizing Amer-
program. ica's machine-tool stock to
bring it to the average level of
Japan's.

Seventy-five percent of = $263 million = President Reagan's proposed
the cost overrun, to 1981, fiscal 1981 and 1982 cuts in the
on the Navy's 5-inch Northeast rail-corridor im-
guided projectile pro- provement programs, and in the
gram. alcohol-fuels development pro-
gram.

Two nuclear-powered aircraft carriers.	= $ 5.8 billion =	the cost of converting 77 oil-using power plants to coal, saving 350,000 barrels of oil per day.
Eighty-eight percent of the cost overrun, to 1981, of the Navy's Tomahawk cruise missile.	= $444 million =	President Reagan's proposed fiscal 1981—1982 cuts in the Federal solar-energy budget.
Three Army AH-64 helicopters	= $ 82 million =	100 top-quality, energy-efficient electric trolleys (made in West Germany)
One F-15A airplane	= $ 29 million =	the cost of training 200 engineers to design and produce electric trolleys in the United States.
46 Army heavy (XM-1) tanks.	= $120 million =	500 top-quality buses (West German-made).
The cost overrun, to 1981, on Navy Frigates (F-FG-7)	= $ 5 billion =	the minimum additional annual investment needed to prevent water pollution in the United States from exceeding present standards.
The cost of unjustified noncombat pentagon aircraft.	= $6.8 billion =	six years of capital investment that is needed to rehabilitate New York City transit.
The cost overrun, to 1981, on the Army's heavy-tank (XM-1) program	= $ 13 billion =	the shortfall of capital needed for maintaining water supplies of 150 United States cities for the next 20 years.
The MX missile system, first cost	= $ 34 billion =	the cost of a comprehensive 10-year energy-efficiency effort to save 25 percent to 50 percent of United States oil imports.
Reactivating two World War II mothballed battleships.	= $376 million =	President Reagan's fiscal 1981 and fiscal 1982 cut in energy-conservation investment.
The cost overrun, to 1981, on the Navy's F-18 aircraft program.	= $26.4 billion =	the cost of electrifying 55,000 miles of mainline railroads, and the cost of new locomotives.

The fiscal 1981 nuclear-weapons funding, adding to more than 20,000 on hand.	= $5.06 billion =	eight years of capital cost for rehabilitating New York City's sewers.
The cost of excessive, nonstandardized military aircraft service equipment.	= $300 million =	President Reagan's fiscal 1981 and 1982 reduction in capital grants for mass transit.
The cost overrun, to 1981, of the Army's UH-60A helicopter program.	= $4.7 billion =	the annual capital investment for restoring New York City's roads, bridges, aqueducts, subways, and buses.
One nuclear (SSN-688) attack submarine	= $582 million =	the cost of 100 miles of electrified rail right-of-way.
Ten B-1 bombers	= $ 2 billion =	the cost of dredging six Gulf Coast and Atlantic Coast harbors to handle 15,000-ton cargo vessels.
One A-6E Intruder (attack plane).	= $ 23 million =	the annual cost of a staff of 200 to plan mutual reversal of the arms race, and conversion of the military economy to a civilian economy.

SCIENTISTS AGREE:
NO ONE CAN WIN A NUCLEAR WAR
Dr. Frederic Solomon and Dr. Mary Coleman
Reprinted from *The Miami Herald,* 11 March 1980.

A belief that the United States should be able to win an all-out nuclear war with the Soviet Union appears to be one foundation of George Bush's approach to military and foreign policy. He rejects the idea that nuclear war has no winners. Bush foresees "survivability" of industrial potential, command and control functions, and a "percentage of the citizens" — even if "everybody fires everything he has" in a nuclear exchange.

As physicians, we are dismayed and alarmed by these pronouncements of a respected political leader, because current medical knowledge shows Bush's assumptions to be dead wrong.

Earlier this month, a group of distinguished physicians and natural scientists met in Cambridge to review the medical consequences of nuclear weapons and nuclear war. The symposium was co-sponsored by the Harvard and Tufts medical schools and Physicians for Social Responsibility. At the conference, renowned authorities documented the futility of medical disaster planning for nuclear war. Effective civil defense and ecological recovery were likewise shown to be essentially impossible.

Consider this information, presented at the symposium:

The single bomb dropped on Hiroshima had the explosive force of about 15 kilotons (15,000 tons of TNT). Nuclear weapons in present-day arsenals range in size from one kiloton to 20 megatons (20 million tons of TNT). Today the United States has over 30,000 nuclear bombs, and the Soviet Union has 20,000.

In an all-out nuclear exchange, all major population and industrial centers would be hit, both in the United States and the Soviet Union. Such an exchange could be complete in one hour. At least 90 percent of the population of both countries would die as a direct result of the thermonuclear blast and radiation.

The survivors, many of them blind and grievously injured, would have to cope with an environmental and ecological catastrophe. Worldwide fallout would contaminate the earth for thousands of years. Plant and bacterial mutations, the disappearance of most birds and mammals, alterations in the earth's temperature, and other atmospheric changes would result in disease, famine, and floods on an unprecedented scale.

After an all-out nuclear war, most of the ozone layer in the earth's atmosphere would be destroyed, according to Professor Henry Kendall, a physicist at M.I.T. The sun's rays would then become terrifying and dangerous. Anyone in the world whose uncovered skin is exposed to daylight would risk incapacitating sunburn within ten minutes and lethal sunburn within an hour. Skin cancer would become rampant. In the long run, only insects can be assured of survival in such a postwar world.

The Cambridge conferees offered conservative estimates of the effects of one 20-megaton thermonuclear bomb upon one large city. Such a bomb would be 1,000 times more powerful than the bomb used on Hiroshima.

If the bomb exploded on ground level on a clear day it would create a fireball one and a half miles in diameter, with temperatures of 20 million to 30 million degrees Fahrenheit. Every structure and every living thing in the downtown area would be vaporized.

Within a ten-mile radius the blast wave, 180-mph winds, and fire would inflict death or injury on almost every human being. At least 50 percent would die immediately. Even at twenty miles from the explosion, half the population would be either killed or injured by the blast pressure and heat. Thus a single nuclear device would result in tens of thousands of life-threatening burn injuries. The entire United States has intensive-care facilities for fewer than 2,000 such cases.

Many would be killed by random spontaneous fires fueled by oil-storage tanks, natural-gas lines, gasoline, and liquid-natural-gas tanks. These fires might coalesce into an enormous firestorm, 1,200 square miles in area, fanned by 100–200-mph winds, creating temperatures capable of cooking and asphyxiating those in shelters. Altogether, immediate death would come to 2.2 million inhabitants of a metropolitan area like Boston with a population of three million.

Survivors of the fires would be exposed to lethal or sublethal doses of radiation from short-term fallout. Even mild winds of twenty miles per hour would carry fallout as far as one hundred fifty miles, where everyone exposed would receive a lethal dose within twenty-four hours. This would cause incurable acute-radiation sickness, with decreased resistance to infection, and inevitable death within one or two weeks. Sublethal doses would produce stillbirths, fetal malformations, leukemia, and cancer. In subsequent generations, if any survived, genetic damage would appear.

Hospitals would be destroyed, and most medical personnel would be among the dead and injured. There would be millions of corpses. Food, air, and water would be contaminated. Survivors would die soon from starvation, dehydration, radiation sickness, and infections.

These estimates are for only one bomb. Population centers are known to be targeted with many bombs. Yet some political leaders still talk confidently of "winning" a nuclear war, including one in which, as George Bush puts it, "everyone fires everything he has."

THE CIA'S TRAGIC ERROR
Arthur Macy Cox

Reprinted from *The New York Review of Books,* 6 November 1980.

Four years ago Jimmy Carter talked about banning nuclear weapons and cutting the defense budget by $7 billion a year. Today he promises to develop the capacity to fight limited nuclear wars and to increase defense spending each year. Detente and arms control are almost dead. The hawks in Moscow are reinforcing the predilections of the hawks in Washington and vice versa. Most of the American advocates of negotiation, and a balance of forces with the USSR, such as Cyrus Vance, Paul Warnke, Leslie Gelb, Marshall Shulman, and Andrew Young, have resigned. Zbigniew Brzezinski is ascendant. If Reagan wins, people who think like Brzezinski will continue to hold power.

This has happened partly because Soviet policymakers have made it possible. Soviet support for the intervention of foreign combat forces in Angola, Ethiopia, Cambodia, and South Yemen was obviously inconsistent with detente. The Soviet invasion of Afghanistan removed any remaining illusions that there were hopeful prospects for U.S.-Soviet agreements. This use of Soviet combat forces showed that the Russians were willing to risk direct intervention in territory beyond the boundaries established by World War II, much as the United States had done when its combat forces were sent to Vietnam.

Even when detente was launched at the Moscow summit in 1972 the Soviets made clear their intent to support liberation movements in the Third World. But no American political leader would have accepted a concept of detente which acquiesced to intervention by combat forces from the outside. The Russians clearly went beyond the understandings of Nixon and Kissinger. These Third World adventures have been combined with a steady buildup of Soviet military forces. The Soviet Union, as we are continually reminded, will soon be capable of threatening the survival of our ground-launched ICBMs.

It has not been difficult, under these circumstances, for the American hawks to have their way. They long for the return of U.S. nuclear superiority that would allow the threat of nuclear confrontation to force the Soviets to back down — the kind of threat that is widely claimed to have worked in the Cuban missile crisis. Even though some hard-liners acknowledge that nuclear superiority may not be attainable again in any meaningful sense, they believe that by exploiting our technological advantages we can exert decisive political pressure on the Soviet system.

American polemicists, with Soviet help, have succeeded in creating an atmosphere in which Soviet strength is consistently and sometimes hysterically exaggerated. The origins of much of this exaggeration can be traced back to December 1976, three weeks before Carter's inauguration, when the newspapers featured disturbing leaked reports about rising Soviet military strength. This was the so-called "Team B" estimate. George Bush, the CIA director at that time, had appointed a panel of ten military experts and Soviet specialists from outside the government to review the CIA's own estimates of Soviet military power and intentions. Led by Richard Pipes, a professor of Russian history at Harvard, Team B was chosen to reflect a tough-minded approach to the USSR. Among its members were retired Army Lieutenant General Daniel O. Graham, the former head of the Pentagon's Defense Intelligence Agency; Paul H. Nitze, former deputy-secretary of defense; Thomas Wolfe, a Soviet military affairs expert at RAND; and William R. Van Cleave, professor of international relations at the University of Southern California.

Team B, after working at the CIA for about three months, vigorously challenged the analysis of Team A, the regular CIA staff charged with estimating Soviet strength. George Bush adopted the Team B findings as the official CIA estimate. In an interview with *The New York Times,* he said that "new evidence and reinterpretation of old information contributed to the reassessment of Soviet intentions." The most important new information available to Team B was the CIA's assessment of Soviet defense spending, published in October 1976, which concluded that the percentage of Soviet gross national product absorbed by defense had jumped from 6 to 8 percent to 11 to 13 percent. The national press and television reported that the CIA had doubled its estimate of Soviet defense spending.

The text of the Team B CIA estimate has never been released, but the leaked story concluded that the USSR was moving ahead of the United States in military strength. The members of Team B asserted that the Soviets were developing the capacity to fight a nuclear war because they had worked out a strategy based on preparing and winning a "limited nuclear war." In an interview with *The Washington Post,* General Graham said that there had been "two.catalytic factors, quite aside from the Team B effort, which had shaped the appraisal of Soviet intentions." One was the CIA estimate recalculating the percentage of Soviet GNP expended for defense. The other major factor in changing the official U.S. perception, Graham said, was "the discovery of a very important Soviet civil defense effort."

According to *The New York Times,* Team B analysts claimed that "the scope and detail of the Soviet civil defense program shows that it is clearly intended as an element in overall military superiority ensuring the survival of Soviet society against the principal adversary, the United States." They maintain that the Soviet civil defense program is further evidence that the Soviets are positioning themselves to fight a nuclear war and still survive as a workable society.

Four years later the views of Team B have become even more influential than they were in 1976 and more in need of scrutiny. For all its conclusions are either wrong, or distorted, or based on misinterpretation of the facts. Many of them have been inadequately challenged by the Carter Administration, or not challenged at all. Along with the Soviet military buildup and the violations of detente I have mentioned, the Team B arguments have had enormous consequences for U.S. defense spending. Paul Nitze and several other members of Team B organized the "Committee on the Present Danger" which has become one of the most powerful lobbies for a larger military establishment. Today Richard Pipes and other members of Team B have joined their former sponsor, George Bush, and are serving as senior advisers to Ronald Reagan.

On civil defense, at least, the Carter Administration has rejected the conclusions of Team B. Interviewed on television on August 17, 1980, Secretary of Defense Harold Brown said: "I don't think massive civil defense programs are going to succeed in protecting the population of countries that try it. I think that the Soviet civil defense program, although it probably is ten times as big as ours, would not, in my judgment, prevent Soviet industry or a great fraction of the Soviet population from being destroyed in an all-out thermonuclear war .... In a limited (nuclear) war if you target cities they are not going to be saved by civil defense."

Here Brown reflects the conclusions of the CIA estimate published in 1979, which concludes that civil defense could not protect enough of the Soviet people and economy to maintain a viable society after an all-out nuclear attack. The Soviets themselves acknowledge that civil defense measures would provide little protection against the U.S. nuclear arsenal. They maintain that their civil defense is primarily for the purpose of providing some protection in the case of war with China. They note that Chinese nuclear weapons are currently so limited that civil defense can still be reasonably effective against them. The United States continues to budget about $100 million a year for civil defense, but most of it is to be used for disaster relief in the case of floods, earthquakes, volcanic eruptions, etc.

Undoubtedly, the members of Team B made their greatest impact on public opinion with the claim that the Soviet Union had doubled its defense spending during the 1970s. Most members of Congress believe this today. So, it seems, do most editorial writers. The CIA's revision has become part of the conventional wisdom of defense policy. A recent study published by the U.S. Air Force and prepared by the U.S. Strategic Studies Institute said: "Estimates prepared by the Central Intelligence Agency, as well as by U.S. academic economists, have been in error by as much as 100 percent. The CIA estimates were accepted without question until 1976, when they were acknowledged to be grossly in error and doubled. Economists have not yet recovered from the shock of that experience."

Similarly, Richard Nixon in his new book, *The Real War,* writes:

> In 1976 the CIA estimates of Russian military spending for 1970–1975 were doubled overnight as errors were discovered and corrected . . . . When the first concrete steps toward arms control were taken, American presidents were being supplied by the CIA with figures on Russian military spending that were only half of what the agency later decided spending had been. Thanks, in part, to this intelligence blunder we will find ourselves looking down the nuclear barrel in the mid-1980s.

But Nixon, Team B, the Congress, and the press have been tragically misinformed. While Team B's report of December 1976 remained classified, the CIA's own official report on Soviet defense spending of October 1976 had contradicted Team B's conclusions, not supported them. The true meaning of the October report has been missed. A gargantuan error has been allowed to stand uncorrected all these years. Here is the CIA's explanation for its change of estimates, as published in the 1976 report: "The new estimate of the share of defense in the Soviet GNP is almost twice as high as the 6 to 8 percent previously estimated. This does not mean that the impact of defense programs on the Soviet economy has increased — only that our appreciation of this impact has changed. *It also implies that Soviet defense industries are far less efficient than formerly believed.*" (Emphasis added.)

So while the CIA increased its estimate of the percentage of Soviet GNP spent on defense from 6 to 8 percent to 11 to 13 percent, there had in fact been no doubling of the rate of actual defense spending. During the period between 1973 and 1976, as CIA analysts refined their methodology and obtained better intelligence, they made an important discovery. In assessing the cost of Soviet defense production they had been crediting the Soviets with a degree of industrial efficiency close to that of the United States. What they discovered was, that Soviet defense production, in fact, was not very efficient. Thus, the Soviet defense effort was absorbing a greater share of the GNP than previously believed. What should have been cause for jubilation became the inspiration for misguided alarm.

In fact, there have been no dramatic increases in Soviet defense spending during the entire decade. In its official estimate, published in January 1980, the CIA concluded as follows for the 1970–1979 period: "Estimated in constant dollars, Soviet defense activities increased at an average annual rate of 3 percent." In other words, the Soviets have indeed been increasing their defense budget, each year, at about the same rate as the United States and most of its NATO partners have raised their military spending, during each of the past four years. The U.S. defense budget for next year calls for an increase, in real terms, of about 5 percent.

Much has been made, also, of the latest CIA study, which shows the total cost of Soviet defense activities for 1979 as 50 percent higher than the U.S. total in dollars, or 30 percent higher in rubles. For example, in his August speech to the Veterans of Foreign Wars, Reagan said, ". . . we're already in an arms race, but only the Soviets are racing. They are outspending us in the military field by 50 percent, and more than double, sometimes triple, on their strategic forces." These figures have very little relation to reality because of the dubious methods used by the CIA. The CIA obtains the dollar cost of Soviet defense by estimating what it would cost the United States to pay for the Soviet defense establishment. The Soviets have 4.4 million people in their armed forces, the United States has 2.1 million. Here is how the CIA estimates the costs of Soviet military personnel:

> We obtain these manpower costs by applying U.S. factors for pay and allowances to our estimates of Soviet military manpower. Soviet military personnel performing duties similar to those of U.S. counterparts are assigned the *same rate of pay* as their counterparts. (Emphasis added.)

But U.S. military personnel are all volunteers with relatively high levels of pay and allowances. The Soviet forces, on the other hand, are mainly conscripted and are paid at about one-fifth the U.S. rate.

The CIA so far has not publicly confronted the obvious distortions caused by these discrepancies. Neither have Reagan and his advisers or members of the Carter Administration. (Similarly, when Reagan claims the USSR spends twice or three times as much as the United States on its strategic forces, he evidently relied on a similar formula by which Soviet costs for executive personnel, factory workers, research staff, computer technicians, etc., are all calculated as if they are paid at relatively high U.S. salaries.)

It is surprising, moreover, that this highly misleading formula has not led the CIA to project even higher costs for Soviet defense. The U.S. defense budget for fiscal year 1981 calls for more than 50 percent to be expended on manpower, whether for salaries, allowances, housing, training, medical, or other activities. (This does not include the $13.7 billion paid for military retirement.) If we estimate the cost of the Soviet forces — which comprise more than twice as many people as ours — at our own rates, one would expect that the Soviet defense budget would be 100 percent higher than ours. This would seem even more likely when one takes into account the inefficiency of Soviet defense industries, which all experts now agree produce weapons at a much higher cost than ours.

Clearly the CIA's method of comparing costs is dangerously deceptive and does not provide an adequate basis for either Congress or the public to assess defense policy. At the same time several other factors should be given much greater emphasis when the administration presents the facts to Congress and the public.

The first is the great difference between the defense contribution made by the European allies of the United States and the Warsaw Pact allies of the Soviet Union. According to the recent report of the International Institute for Strategic Studies,* in 1979 the European members of NATO spent $76 billion for defense and France, a non-NATO ally, spent $20 billion — a total of $96 billion. The Warsaw Pact members other than the USSR spent $17 billion, or less than one-fifth of the defense outlay of our European allies. (In citing these figures, I leave aside the obvious question whether the USSR can count on the loyalty of local Warsaw Pact troops in Poland, Hungary, and Czechoslovakia.)

Perhaps even more important in considering relative military burdens are the Soviet costs related to China. The U.S. Defense Department says: "At least 22 percent of the increase in the Soviet defense budget during these years (1964–1977) has been attributed to the buildup in the Far East . . . . The high construction costs in Siberia suggest that the intelligence estimates may understate the cost of the Soviet buildup in the Far East substantially." In addition, according to the Defense Department, the Soviets "station as much as 25 percent of their ground forces and tactical air power on their border with China."

The Soviet costs in connection with China come more sharply in focus when we observe that the Soviets have forty-four divisions facing China and thirty divisions facing NATO. Of the thirty divisions in Central Europe, four are standing guard in Hungary and five have remained in Czechoslovakia since the invasion of 1968. In other words, there are about twice as many divisions committed to the China front as to the West German front.

Furthermore, the United States does not have to match the Soviet forces facing China. These forces are at the end of a long and tenuous line of communication that can be severed, in time of war, by missile strikes. These are not forces that can be steadily transferred to combat in a European war. On the other hand, if it is argued that the U.S. defense budget should provide forces to counter the Soviet threat to China, then the Chinese defense budget should be included on our side — a total of $50 billion.

The combined NATO defense budgets are greater than the combined Soviet-Warsaw Pact defense budgets, and if the China factor is included, the Soviet proportion of defense facing the United States and its allies is less than 75 percent of that of the NATO powers. The claim of Soviet military superiority is an illusion based, in large part, on a misunderstanding of the facts. As the

* *The Military Balance, 1980–1981,* The International Institute for Strategic Studies, 23 Tavistock Street, London WC2E7NQ.

Defense Department recently said in commenting on the 1980–1981 report of the International Institute for Strategic Studies in London, "The Soviets may have made impressive strides in upgrading their land-based nuclear missiles, but . . . the United States remains superior in submarine and bomber-launched nuclear weapons." As for conventional power, "The Communist bloc may have more conventional weapons, such as tanks, but the West is ahead in counter weapons such as antitank missiles. The result is that both sides are about equal in total military power."

The conclusion of Team B that has perhaps the most ominous continuing consequences is the finding that Soviet strategic theory has been different from ours — because the Soviets are said to believe that nuclear wars can actually be fought and that limited nuclear wars are a real possibility. Both Carter and Reagan have adopted dangerous doctrines based on this mistaken analysis.

In a tortuous speech at the Naval War College on August 20, Harold Brown attempted to explain Presidential Directive 59, which accepts the concept of fighting limited nuclear wars and provides authority to build the weapons necessary to carry out that concept. Brown said:

> Soviet leadership appears to contemplate at least the possibility of a relatively prolonged (nuclear) exchange if a war comes, and in some circles at least, they seem to take seriously the theoretical possibility of victory in such a war . . . . The increase in Soviet strategic capability over the past decade, and our concern that the Soviets may not believe that nuclear war is unwinnable, dictate a U.S. need for more — and more selective — retaliatory options.

Brown, however, made clear his own views on retaliatory limited warfare in his annual report to Congress this year, in which he said:

> In adopting and implementing this policy we have no more illusions than our predecessors that a nuclear war could be closely and surgically controlled. There are, of course, great uncertainties about what would happen if nuclear weapons were ever used again . . . My own view remains that a full-scale thermonuclear exhange would constitute an unprecedented disaster for the Soviet Union and for the United States. And I am not at all persuaded that what started as a demonstration, or even a tightly controlled use of strategic forces for larger purposes, could be kept from escalating to a full-scale thermonuclear exchange.

It is true that articles in Soviet military journals have discussed the strategy and tactics of nuclear war. Soviet military leaders say that if they are attacked with nuclear weapons they will fight and win a nuclear war. In this they do not seem different from generals elsewhere. U.S. military planners are constantly engaged in war games in which nuclear wars are fought on paper, and through computers, and in the end are won. When Brown said on August 20 that Soviet leaders take seriously the theoretical possibility of victory, he might also have noted the statement of his own chairman of the Joint Chiefs of Staff, made as long ago as 1977:

> U.S. nuclear strategy maintains military strength sufficient to deter attack, but also in the event deterence fails, sufficient to provide a warfighting capability to respond to a wide range of conflict in order to control escalation and terminate the war on terms acceptable to the United States.

Neither Soviet nor U.S. leaders, however, have ever talked about launching a first strike to win nuclear war; nor have the leaders of either country threatened such a strike for coercive political purposes. Brezhnev has explicitly rejected the concept of limited nuclear war: "I am convinced," he has said, "that even one nuclear bomb dropped by one side over the other would result in general nuclear exchange — a nuclear holocaust not only for our two nations, but for the entire world . . . . The starting of a nuclear war would spell annihilation for the aggressor himself." Despite Team B and the rhetoric of the presidential campaign, both countries still can be said to follow the principles of deterrence and of avoiding a direct confrontation that would lead to a nuclear exchange.

Both Brezhnev and Carter, moreover, claim that the two strategic forces are equal. Harold Brown, in his speech at the end of August, confirmed that "we have essential equivalence now." But if the Soviets continue to deploy more MIRVs on their missiles, and if we move ahead with a new round of strategic systems including the MX missile, the strategic balance may well be lost.

The better course would be to start, after the November elections, a new round of negotiations. While these are taking place, both sides should agree to freeze deployment of any additional strategic weapons and to do so while they are essentially equal in such weapons. Brezhnev has stated not only that he is eager to engage in negotiations, including limitations on medium-range nuclear weapons in Europe, but that he is ready to sign an agreement banning all nuclear testing, and providing for on-site verification. The United States would be foolish not to explore these possibilities. Once such an agreement was signed, it would be very difficult to develop new nuclear weapons, because they cannot be relied upon unless they can be tested and demonstrated to be effective.

The opportunities for genuine arms control are still very real ones. The prospects for successful negotiation become better the more clearly both sides understand that one alternative is the growing possibility of accidental nuclear disaster. George Kistiakowsky, one of the world's leading authorities on nuclear weapons and former science adviser to President Dwight Eisenhower, recently said: "Given the present geopolitical trends and the quality of the political leaders that burden mankind, it would be a miracle if no nuclear warheads exploded by the end of this century and only a bit smaller miracle if that did not lead to a nuclear holocaust." There is not much time to continue to indulge the kind of irrational politics we have witnessed, on both sides, during the last few years.

WHAT MAKES A WAR "JUST"?
Edward LeRoy Long, Jr.
Reprinted from *The Christian Science Monitor,* 10 February 1981.

My purpose here is to illumine the issues germane to the "just war" theory — not to advocate its adoption.

The criteria traditionally advanced by the just war theory divide into two groups: the first delineating the conditions under which it is legitimate to make war; the second specifying the kinds of actions that may legitimately be employed.

Heading the first group is the criterion of "last resort": all other means of reconciling a conflict must be exhausted before armed conflict can be morally legitimized. Generally speaking, most Americans are genuinely prepared to accept this criterion as standard practice.

Second, in order to be just, a war must be explicitly declared by a competent authority. The requirement means that a nation-state has to announce that it has exhausted other means of seeking redress and is targeting a specific opponent. This keeps the process — or would if it were taken as binding — from treachery and deceit. It requires war — in a certain profound sense — to be honorable.

Third, a war can be morally just only if it has "a reasonable chance of success." That sounds crudely opportunistic, as though a war can be justified only if it can be won. But there is a profound truth at stake.

Certainly it is irrational to engage in war if it cannot possibly attain the objectives for which it is professed to be fought. If one went to war only to prove some macho self-image, or to be a hero, or to embrace martyrdom, the ethical stance would be quite different from that in just-war teaching. War undertaken for such reasons would be an instrument of self-will, or group will, but not a means of achieving meaningful social consequences.

This criterion has been given a good deal of attention in the atomic age. How can push-button atomic war possibly have a reasonable chance of success? If deterrence doesn't work, are we then to blow up an enemy as a kind of punitive retaliation for starting something? Punitive retaliation by itself would be an insufficient ground for a just war.

Fourth, in order for war to be just it must be undertaken with the right intentions; it must seek to correct some wrong or achieve some protection for righteousness and order. This criterion allows some taking of risks for the sake of results, elevating the calculative prudentiality of reasonable success to a good-faith effort that can be made in the face of odds. What it rules out is war to express vindictive anger, to purge feelings of hostility, or to parade prowess.

A hypothetical response to the [recent] hostage situation in Iran shows how these criteria would restrain certain kinds of action. Suppose in the first flush of dismay and anger over the taking of the hostages we had begun saturation bombing of Tehran. Such an action would have failed the tests of just war; it would not have been a last resort; it would have been done as a result of an explicit declaration of intent; it would not have succeeded in solving the hostage problem, because the hostages would have been destroyed in the process. It would have been more a venting of national fury.

Just-war teaching applies other criteria to conflict after it begins.

The first of these is something called the principle of proportionality. Actions taken in war must be commensurate with their consequences. You don't keep your neighbor from borrowing your wheelbarrow by shooting off his arms. Just as one is not justified in going to war unless there is some chance of accomplishing social and political objectives, so one is not justified, once war has begun, in using strategies that are utterly disproportionate in destructive consequences to one's strategic aims.

This principle is quite understandable when applied to wartime strategies. It is more complex when applied to means of deterrence which, if used, would be as disastrous to the user as to the enemy. It may be we are using for deterrence threats to employ weapons that cannot possibly pass the test of proportionality. In doing so, we may be saying we have no intention of taking just-war criteria seriously, or we may simply be hoping the bluff will work.

The final criterion of just war is the recognition of the immunity of noncombatants. This criterion appears increasingly problematic in view of modern weaponry. How can it be applied under conditions of saturation bombing? Would it have any significance at all in an atomic conflagration?

Perhaps the just-war criteria postulate a world that does not exist, if so — if the international arena is truly a jungle of secrecy, willful malfeasance, and brutal drives — the criteria may be quaintly irrelevant. But then also is the expectation that anyone will regard anyone else as worthy of respect, trust, or honor.

COUNTERING THE THEORY OF
LIMITED NUCLEAR WAR
John C. Bennett
Reprinted from *The Christian Century,* 7 January 1981.

A new situation in regard to the possession and possible use of nuclear weapons has crept up on the American people. The axiom that formerly prevailed — that we possess nuclear weapons only to prevent their use — is gradually losing force, and now many persons close to the centers of decision-making have the idea that we should be prepared actually to use our nuclear weapons in the hope of coming out ahead of any adversary.

I was first made aware of this gradual shift when I read an article by Leon Sigal in *Foreign Policy* (Spring 1979) in which he describes two schools of thought in the Pentagon — the "stable balancers," who still believe in possessing nuclear weapons to prevent their use, and the "war-fighting" school. At that time Sigal thought that the first group was in the majority, but since then an increasing acceptance of the second position seems to have developed in the context of belief in the possibility of limited nuclear wars. This idea was given special emphasis in the general discussion of the new presidential directive for nuclear strategy (Directive 59) limiting use of these weapons to targeting the nuclear forces and installations of the adversary.

This change of mind in the Pentagon about the use of nuclear weapons gives the American churches a chance to come to a much clearer and more forceful position on nuclear weapons and nuclear war than has generally been the case. Many initiatives in the churches have called attention to the need to control the arms race, and both Roman Catholic teaching and ecumenical teaching in the context of the World Council of Churches have been clear in seeing nuclear war, or any other form of total war, to be in absolute conflict with Christian faith. But in U.S. churches one conflict has not been well articulated — that of absolute pacifists and nuclear pacifists on the one hand (those who cannot justify the possession of nuclear weapons and who by implication favor unilateral nuclear disarmament), and those on the other hand who have reluctantly accepted the view that the possession of nuclear weapons in a structure of mutual nuclear deterrence is the surest way under present conditions to prevent nuclear war. Today, in view of the recent changes in government thinking, it should be possible for both groups in the churches to work together in opposition to the limited-nuclear-war theorists.

A new factor affecting decision-making is the development of a community of nuclear experts who live in a world of their own that others do not understand. The distinction between the nuclear specialists and those outside the field differs from the more familiar contrast between the role of the military and that of civilians. These experts spend their lives designing nuclear weapons, projecting nuclear strategies, and dreaming about the scenarios of nuclear war. They may as civilians occupy "think tanks," and they may either as civilians or as members of the military work in the Pentagon.

In a recent article Lord Solly Zuckerman, former chief scientific adviser to the British government, writes about the situation with which he was familiar in his country:

> The men in the nuclear weapons laboratories on both sides have succeeded in creating a world with an arrational foundation, on which a new set of political realities has in turn been built. They have become the alchemists of our times, working in secret ways which cannot be divulged, casting spells which embrace us all.
>
> Weekly *Manchester Guardian,* October 19, 1980.

He adds that "the more destructive power there is, one must assume they imagine, the greater chance of military success." Political leaders are likely to take many more facts and values into account, and this has often been true of military leaders as well, but there is a danger that such leaders may listen to these nuclear experts with their specialized vision, and perhaps in making desperate decisions trust the specialists' judgment about limited nuclear war. Fortunately there is a large and independent scientific community which can warn us all against arcane judgments.

Quite apart from Directive 59, the idea of limited nuclear war has been considered by those who think in terms of using tactical nuclear weapons in situations far from our shores, where we might be at a disadvantage because of lack of conventional weapons capability. It seems to be taken for granted that, if we were losing in a confrontation with the Soviet Union in any part of the world, we would use tactical nuclear weapons, perhaps initiating their use to save us from defeat. Such an instance seems to pose the greatest danger of our getting involved in nuclear war — a situation where we would be "backing into it."

But doesn't the Soviet Union also have tactical nuclear weapons? If their use were stepped up on both sides, what chance would there be of keeping the war limited, since the important barrier to escalation — the nuclear threshold — would have been crossed? Also, one side or the other might then attack in another part of the world where its strength was greater and by this route lead to a great enlargement of the war with unforeseen consequences.

The strategy of Directive 59 would be less limited in its effects than is usually recognized. Nuclear experts admit that there would be millions of casualties, between 10 million and 20 million in the country first targeted, and since it is doubtful that the target country's retaliatory force could be fully destroyed, there would probably be millions of casualties on the other side. What is almost never said is that thousands of nuclear explosions, *whatever their targets,* would have a damaging effect on the atmosphere of the whole northern hemisphere. Does anyone know — or even try to take account of — the extent to which radioactive materials would spread over a continent even when the targets are limited?

A prior consideration is that the very policy of preparation to strike the nuclear forces of the other side involves a first-strike capability that becomes a temptation for the other side to strike first, perhaps against cities, thus making nuclear war more likely than it is now.

There is no way of stretching Christian ethics, or any other humane ethics, to justify such preparations or to justify the initiation of nuclear war, even if the intention is to keep it limited. There are only two ways to think of war in Christian terms. One is the way of the pacifist minority, which has some influence on the sensitivities of others. The other way is to recognize that some uses of military force are justified, but always on the condition that they be limited — limited in their effect on noncombatants, limited by the possibility of perceiving strong chances that the war would make possible a better peace.

The Second Vatican Council spoke for the ecumenical Christian conscience when it said: "Any act of war aimed indiscriminately at the destruction of entire cities or extensive areas along with their population is a crime against God and man himself." Catholic teaching about the criteria for justified war allows for a "double effect" and recognizes that even when the main target is military, many noncombatants are likely to be in the neighborhood and to be victims. Hence there must be some sense of proportionality in justifying the military action by relating the number of "side-effect" victims to the purpose of the action. But when the side effect consists of 10 million to 20 million casualties, many of them noncombatants, there is no possibility of justifying the action. Nuclear war would produce in addition many indirect or delayed side effects which have never entered into the traditional discussion of the "just" and "unjust" war.

The side effects to which I shall now turn should be lifted up for emphasis in the churches partly because they are generally neglected and partly because they clearly mark the difference between nuclear war and previous forms of war. The latter consideration is important because one aspect of the current changes in military philosophy is a tendency to say that nuclear weapons are just an extension of other means of fighting. It would be well to reflect on the fact that, horrible as World War II was in its destructiveness, the nations most devastated have in large measure been restored. The prosperity and political health of both Germany and Japan illustrate this regeneration.

As for the indirect and delayed effects of nuclear war, there would first be the struggle of the survivors to bury the dead and to find their way across radioactive soil to find food and medical care. How many doctors and nurses would have survived?* How many survivors would even in the early stages become victims of hopeless illnesses?

If there were thousands of nuclear explosions in two countries, the effect on the atmosphere would be serious regardless of the targets. A report of the United States Arms Control and Disarmament Agency titled "Worldwide Effects of Nuclear War," as quoted by Francis X. Winters (in *Ethics and Nuclear Strategy,* by Harold P. Ford [Orbis, 1977], p. 147), gives the following estimates of the effect on the atmosphere of an all-out nuclear war:

> Such a war would destroy 30 to 70 percent of the ozone layer in the entire northern hemisphere and between 20 and 40 percent of it in the southern hemisphere as well. The destruction of the ozone layer would have truly apocalyptic consequences, such as a two- to three-year destruction of agriculture (because of a change of even one degree in the average temperature), disabling sunburn or snow blindness, and disruption of communications.

A counter force war that did not target the cities might have a somewhat reduced effect, but how much less destructive it would be we do not know; and in any case there is no good reason to be optimistic that a limited war could be kept limited in a time of desperation.

How great would be the increase of hunger in this country and on other continents as a side effect of nuclear war? How much of the radioactive land would be uninhabitable and for how long? I recall that when there was talk of a possible meltdown at Three Mile Island, it was assumed that after such an

---

* See "Scientists Agree: No One Can Win a Nuclear War," p. 94.

accident, a large area of Pennsylvania would be uninhabitable for some time. How would thousands of intended nuclear explosions compare in their effect with one such accident?

How many of the survivors could expect to have cancer in ten or twenty years? What would be the genetic effects of so many explosions on the children and later descendants of the survivors? How far have military or political planners gone in trying to get answers to such questions? What right have the decision-makers of this generation to deprive future generations of so much of the material and cultural capital that they should be able to inherit?

Another side effect of nuclear war would be the impact on the morale of the world, especially that part of the world most visited by destruction, as well as the morale of onlookers, perhaps in the southern hemisphere, who could well despair of the reason and conscience of the human race and fear for their own future.

Two political realists have stressed the importance for our nation to be ready to use power, including military power in some situations: theologian Reinhold Niebuhr and Hans Morgenthau, the most renowned of American political scientists who emphasized international relations. Niebuhr wrote of nuclear war: "Could a civilization loaded with this monstrous guilt have enough moral health to survive?" (*Christianity and Crisis,* 13 November 1961).

Morgenthau declared that only a person "who is possessed not only by extreme optimism but by an almost unthinking faith" can believe "that civilization, any civilization, Western or other, could survive such an unprecedented catastrophe" (*Commentary,* October 1961). He even went so far as to say that such a war would destroy for the secularist without a transcendent faith the meaning of life. He added that it would destroy even the meaning of death, as it would rob death of all individuality. Said Morgenthau: "The possibility of nuclear death, by destroying the meaning of life and death, has reduced to absurd cliches the noble words of yesterday. To defend freedom and civilization is absurd when to defend them amounts to destroying them" ("Death in the Nuclear Age," *Commentary,* September 1961).

One might try to reduce the impact of these words by saying that Morgenthau had in mind an all-out nuclear war and that they might not apply fully to the more limited counterforce war in the minds of some of our military planners. Quite apart from the fact that a limited nuclear war would not be as limited as is usually suggested, there is the great risk that it would lead to an all-out war. Shortly before his death, Morgenthau wrote: "The use of nuclear weapons, even if at first on a limited scale, would unleash unmitigated disaster, which could lead to the destruction of both belligerents" (*New Republic,* 20 October 1979).

I think that this political scientist is a better guide than the nuclear experts and military planners. We should add to what he said that many nonbelligerent neighbors would be caught in the cross fire; they too would suffer from any damage done to the atmosphere. In our American discussion this fact is seldom mentioned, and it should receive special attention in the churches.

In defense of what interests and values would all this destruction be wrought?

At present we can easily imagine that we might become involved in nuclear war for the sake of oil or for the sake of freedom. In either case, it would be self-defeating. Such a war would probably destroy the oil wells and installations so that they would be unusable for a long time, and it would destroy the industrial civilization that needs so much oil.

Moreover, the institutions of freedom would probably be among the casualties. Survivors trying to put their world together again would require authoritarian government, and there would be a serious break in the continuity of institutions and traditions. One can imagine how difficult it would be to restore the precious and precarious traditions of freedom.

Herbert Butterfield, British diplomatic historian and lay theologian, put the matter very well: "With modern weapons we could easily put civilization back a thousand years, while the course of a single century can produce a colossal transition from despotic regimes to a system of liberty" (*International Conflict in the Twentieth Century — A Christian View,* by Herbert Butterfield [Harper, 1960]).

If the churches are loyal to the purposes of God as known through Christ for humanity and for this earth, they will give major — and that means much-increased — attention to the prevention of nuclear war. This task will involve exerting pressure on both public opinion and government when either is tempted to become carelessly confrontational or belligerent; it will also involve continuous pressure for control of the arms race, leading to radical reduction of armaments. Today there is more talk about linkage between arms control and other issues related to the Soviet Union. I hope that the new administration will not push this concept too far, because arms control is in the interest of the security of both superpowers, quite apart from other considerations. Also, since it would reduce the danger of nuclear war, it is in the interests of everyone.

As a nonpacifist (though no hawk!) who assumes that we cannot dispense with the use of power, sometimes military power, in international relations, I would raise the question whether the concerns expressed in this article might inhibit all use of military force regardless of the provocation and regardless of what values might be at stake in particular situations. My answer is "No," but these concerns do mean that there would be a heavier burden of proof on the use of military power than formerly.

The clearest imperative is that we should avoid initiating a nuclear stage in what is supposed to be a limited war. I doubt that we would ever be tempted to use such weapons to initiate a nuclear war, though we cannot put that beyond possibility if military and political planners became convinced that they could, by a "limited" first strike, destroy the capacity of the other side to retaliate. That would be a terrible wrong in itself because of the inevitable side effects and the number of innocent people who would be immediately wounded or killed. It would be an appalling case of political recklessness.

There will be need of more cool-headedness and political skill among policymakers than ever before, and among both policymakers and public there will be a need for commitments, for sensitivity and prudence, and for a willingness to take account of the fears and insecurities of the other side. The overarching fact in this context is that nuclear war itself is the greatest threat to the superpowers, to their neighbors, and to all people.

PEACEMAKING IN THE PARISHES
Richard G. Watts
Reprinted from *The Christian Century,* 8 April 1981.

Is a new peace movement about to take root in the churches? There are some signs indicating that the answer may be Yes. It is not simply that the historic peace churches — Friends, Mennonite, Brethren — are seeking to recover their heritage in depth through a "New Call to Peacemaking." Mainline churches are also awakening to the threat of an unbridled arms race, and to the realization that nuclear war is becoming "thinkable." The Riverside Church Disarmament Conferences have spun off more than two hundred additional local and regional conferences, and 2,500 requests came to Riverside last spring for Peace Sabbath materials. The United Presbyterian Church has adopted a call for emphasis on peacemaking ministries at every level of the church's life over the next four years, and undergirded that emphasis with a special offering to be received each World Communion Sunday.

The key issue, of course, is whether the call to peacemaking will find its way into the center of parish liturgy, community, and mission, or whether it will stay out on the periphery, an extracurricular activity for people interested in that sort of thing.

For the past year I have been coordinating a pilot project in peacemaking ministry among the United Presbyterian churches of northeast Ohio. Out of that experience have come some suggestions about the shape of peace education and action ministries for parishes newly awakening to what George Kennan has called our "countdown to disaster."

The starting point for peace education is consciousness-raising, for most church people, like American citizens generally, are simply unaware of the awesome nuclear mathematics and of the strategic doctrines that make nuclear war thinkable. Nonetheless, people are remarkably open to the message that the arms race must be slowed, stopped, and reversed, and that the time to begin is now. If, as we are told, some 75 percent of the populace supports increased military spending, I argue that that is a very fragile consensus responding to very limited information. Let the people learn a few basic facts:

1. that a single Poseidon submarine can destroy every large and medium-sized city in the Soviet Union (and we have forty-one Polaris and Poseidon submarines);
2. that while a mere 400 or 500 nuclear bombs could destroy two-thirds of the Soviet Union's industry and 40 million of its people, we possess some 11,000 strategic nuclear bombs;
3. that from 1971 to 1977 the United States sold $56 billion worth of arms,

three times the total of the preceding twenty years, and that over 70 percent went to developing nations;

4. that in the mid-70s the Shah of Iran was our number one customer for arms, spending nearly a third of Iran's gross national product on the military by 1975–76;

5. that if one handed the Pentagon a $1,000 bill every hour of every day, it would take over 200,000 years to hand over what we will spend on the military during the 1980s.

Invariably the response to such facts is a shaking of heads and murmurs of "That's crazy!" Laying out the awful arithmetic of the arms race gives people who have been beguiled by words like "defense" and "security" an opportunity to call the craziness by its right name.

The biggest barrier to be overcome is the question "What about the Russians?" George Kennan, former U.S. ambassador to the Soviet Union and an architect of the postwar "containment" policy, has given the best recent answer. Of course the Soviet Union must do its part, he said, but first we need to remove several beams from our own eyes. One is to overcome our "terrible and fateful fascination" with nuclear weapons, which "are really useless precisely because they are too destructive to serve any rational purpose." For another, we must try to repress our peculiarly American tendency to [resort to] the dehumanization of any major national opponent: the tendency, that is, to form a species of devil-image of that opponent, to deprive him in our imaginations of all normal human attributes, and to see him as totally evil and devoted to nothing but our destruction.

To use the church's language, Kennan is pointing out our need to avoid the sin of idolatry, of identifying our nation and our interests with God and so justifying every sort of response to an "ungodly" foe. I have found that, given assurance that peacemaking does not mean simply disarming totally and unilaterally, most people will consider initiatives the United States might take toward disarmament, and are even willing to think about the legitimate security interests of the Soviet Union.

The political realities cannot be sidestepped, and Reinhold Niebuhr's dictum holds: "Consecrated ignorance is still ignorance." Yet education for peacemaking must not be turned into a seminar on international relations. The churches' most potent resource is the Bible, with its testimony to a Kingdom that transcends the kingdoms of this world. It is the vision of that Kingdom of justice, peace, and love, and the occasional experience of it, that sets us free to call into question the prevailing assumptions of the present order of things.

A second step in peacemaking ministry is the formation within the parish of small support groups for study and action. There are three reasons for emphasizing this step. First, we live with a "crisis of the week" mentality; whatever is on the cover of *Time* or *Newsweek* is this week's concern, to be cast aside when next week's issue arrives. People need support over the long haul, for the tough, slogging work of searching out alternatives to war.

Second, support systems are needed by those who confront "principalities and powers" that are bigger than they are. Even David had a cheering section when he took on Goliath. And third, small groups link us together in a faith community where the context of thinking/action about the arms race is Scripture, prayer, and celebration. Without roots in the community of faith, our public efforts are likely to be, as Langdon Gilkey once observed, merely a footnote in a volume of contemporary sociology.

But peacemaking ministry must have as its action goal the changing of national policy; that is the end toward which education and mutual support aim. Changing the extraordinary misallocation of national resources and taking steps to stop the arms race are initiatives for which the government has shown no zeal. But peacemaking ministries surely will have such public-policy goals as these: (1) a moratorium on production and deployment of nuclear weapons; (2) slowing of the arms trade, particularly to Third World nations; (3) transfer of funds from Pentagon budget to domestic human needs; (4) prompt initiatives for a comprehensive SALT treaty; and (5) planning for economic conversion to civilian industry. Whatever the particular goal may be, it cannot be attained unless Christians enter the public-policy arena, so that the shaping of a vision of national security is not left by default to defense-profiting industries and the Pentagon.

There is no reason why a public-advocacy network cannot be formed to carry out "reverse the arms race" efforts. The people who are worried about nuclear holocaust and hoping for alternatives are out there, but they need to be found and organized.

President Eisenhower, who seemed to reflect increasingly on the dangers of the national security state, said shortly before his death: "Above all, . . . I'd like to believe that the people in the long run are going to do more to promote peace than our governments. Indeed, I think that people want peace so much that one of these days governments better get out of their way and let them have it."

In this new mood to shift national policy through impetus from the people, the churches' role is to create a national legislative network that will do for issues of disarmament what Bread for the World has done on hunger. Without such a network, for which congregations across the land will supply their lists of committed persons, the churches' Washington-based lobbyists will continue to be perceived — quite rightly — as (pardon the metaphor) generals without armies.

As a vital part of peacemaking ministry, facilitators on local, presbytery, conference, and district levels can help to fan the flames of the peace movement in the parishes. The pastor, who is the world's last generalist — always juggling eighteen programmatic balls at once and thus unable to keep on top of peacemaking issues and resources — can benefit from people "working the territory." Such people can counsel with concerned pastors and laity, do basic research, spy out and distribute useful resources, and beat the bushes to find new people for that public-policy network. Also, somebody needs to take the time to create ecumenical linkages that can save us from isolation and duplication of effort.

As denominations gear up for peace emphases, they may be tempted to respond by placing a few more staff people in New York and Washington, or even to allocate part of presently available staff time to this new effort. What is required, however, is a significant investment in peace advocates or enablers (or whatever one may choose to call them), working face-to-face with pastors and congregations in their local situation. Broadening of the base of the peace movement can come about only through the "evangelization" of people who have not identified themselves with the churches' pacifists or social activists — through bringing into being a grassroots cry for peace that cannot be denied in Washington.

Alan Geyer, director of the Churches' Center for Theology and Public Policy, has said that "engaging in the struggle to end the nuclear arms race is the clearest command of prophetic faith in our generation." In speaking last spring to a consultation of the National Council of Churches, however, Geyer made it clear that so far the church has evaded that command. And he went on to say:

> I have no doubt that if our own church leaders could be persuaded that their ministry absolutely requires their steadfast involvement in the struggle for disarmament, the political battle for disarmament in this country would be more than half won.
>
> No words on the arms race which ... any Christian body addresses to politicians or military leaders or scientists or industrialists should be uttered with untempered indignation. Not with the churches' own inexcusable sin in failing to make the arms race the target of its own mission and the crucible of its own theology.

There are signs of awakening, but will peacemaking become central to the churches' self-understanding, reflected in liturgy and mission? What is now required of us, along with the setting up of parish programs, is, more centrally, theological reflection upon who we are as the church — those who, hiding behind locked doors, receive the gift of the Holy Spirit from the Lord who says: "Shalom. As the Father sent me, I send you."

THE CHURCH AND THE BOMB
William F. Wolff
Reprinted from *America*, 10 January 1981.

"We Americans are good people," writes W. H. Ferry, "yet we are preparing to commit the most hideous crime in the annals of mankind. Where Hitler murdered millions, we are ready to annihilate hundreds of millions." Worst of all, unlike Hitler's "ordinary Germans," who could claim that they were unaware of the gas ovens, we ordinary Americans are "active co-conspirators" in a national policy that could reduce God's sweet earth into a barren radioactive cinder.

Although several nations have nuclear weapons enough to inflict terrible damage, only the United States and the Soviet Union have the capability of bringing all humanity "to that mournful hour in which it will experience no peace other than the dreadful peace of death." Both we and the Soviets have weapons enough in our individual arsenal to put the world out of its misery, yet, paradoxically, neither of us alone poses a credible threat to human survival. If either the Soviet Union or the United States were to unilaterally destroy its own nuclear arsenal, the danger of either a preemptive or escalated blundering into a final holocaust would disappear.

Faced by what David Riesman has called the "overriding issue" of our time, either we or the Russian people could free the world of the specter of nuclear annihilation, although at an unknown cost to the nation willing to take the gamble. Unfortunately, the nature of Soviet society is such that, in reality, the decision is left to us. We have to decide whether our perceived self-interest outweighs the threat that our perceived self-interest poses to all human survival.

Gary Wills and others have argued that unilateral nuclear disarmament — not to be confused with a total or even partial disarmament — would strengthen, not weaken our nation. Reasonable as such arguments may be, they have gained little currency. The people of the United States have been convinced that they need both a massive military force and nuclear weapons. Neither the military, the political establishment, nor the news media are prepared to disabuse the public of this notion.

In complex issues where reason can be either a crutch or a club, the argument ordinarily goes to the biggest mouth and the strongest arm. If such issues have a moral dimension, however, views sanctioned by a secular authority and the weightiest of interests can be undermined by a seemingly weak opposition. Thus, although great armies of reason and self-interest have been marshaled in support of a public policy favoring abortion on demand, moral claims for the sanctity of human life have enabled a minority, backed in varying degrees by their religious institutions, to mount a reasonably successful holding action against what is purported to be the will of the majority.

A similar but smaller campaign, against the use of nuclear weapons, has met with far less success. This effort, backed by the peace churches and to a very limited extent by the major congregations, has been directed against all warfare on the premise that the next major war will be a nuclear war and that such a war would end in a holocaust. From a Christian perspective, at least, the arguments are impeccable, yet all our political and military leaders plunge ahead in their preparations for this unthinkable war with the full support of a great majority of our people.

The failure of this antinuclear campaign can be attributed to any number of factors. Among these might be included what is seen as a self-righteous moral obtuseness on the part of the American people or their leaders, historical circumstances such as the gradual buildup of our nuclear arsenals, and economic factors such as the jobs of those engaged in the production and care of atomic weapons. To these can be added various tactical failures, the seeming

aloofness of the main religious bodies, and a pervasive sense of despair, a sense
that we are all doomed, that there is nothing we can do. Many of these factors
are truly outside our control, but some can be handled.

First, we can rid ourselves of despair. We should be able to do at least as well
with this problem as with the abortion issue. In the weapons case all innocent
lives are at stake, not just those of the unborn.

Second, we can abandon the all-or-nothing tactic. Much as we would like to
get rid of both war and nuclear weapons, we cannot tie these two issues
together. The great majority of the American people accept the legitimacy of
warfare. Our enormous military budget attests to the fact. Even the Vatican
Council refused to deny the right of nations to legitimate defense, nor did it
call them to "unilateral disarmament." Thus, so long as the only substantive
antinuclear response is that defense will be impossible under such conditions,
the weapons will stay. Accordingly, the antiwar crusade will have to be subordi-
nated to the antinuclear campaign.

Third, the major religious denominations must somehow be dragged, cajoled,
shamed, or otherwise encouraged to work for our country's renunciation of the
nuclear option. Certainly the problem has always belonged with the churches,
yet the Kremlin has preached better sermons on the immorality of nuclear
weapons than have most of our ministers. Now, however, we have come to a
time of reckoning. If the American churches continue to let our country play
nuclear roulette, with all creation at stake, their silence will be a cowardice and
an affront to God no less terrible than the silence of the German church when
His people were herded into the gas chambers of Central Europe.

The Roman Catholic Church, one might hope, will be one of the first to break
this awful silence. Ever since the dawn of the atomic age, popes and the council
have consistently condemned the use of weapons of mass destruction. Fifteen
years ago the council condemned "any act of war aimed . . . at the destruction
of entire cities or of extensive areas . . . with their population" as "crimes
against God and man." Calling the arms race an "utterly treacherous trap,"
the council questioned "where the evil road we have ventured upon will lead
us."

Now, many years down this "evil road," a meaningful response by the
American church is long overdue. The well-meaning but bureaucratic and
almost diffident reaction of our church to this problem is reflected in a recent
article by Edward Doherty. Here, all hope seems to be placed in certain
government initiatives such as the SALT process. SALT III, which will pre-
sumably be signed by a few remaining radioactive cockroaches, is almost
plaintively seen as giving some "hope" of negotiating for the first time significant reactions in weapons levels on both sides.

The logic behind this leave-it-to-the-government stance is somewhat convo-
luted. Seemingly, according to "Catholic moralists" and "the church itself as
a teaching body," nuclear weapons can be used "to deter a war" but probably
not to "wage one." Yet it is acknowledged that any "war between the nuclear
superpowers, even if it begins with conventional forces . . . is likely to end" in
a nuclear war. Thus, the morally licit deterrent weapons will "likely" be used
in an illicit manner.

Such self-contradictory, issue-evading morality can be avoided, however, by allowing Daniel and Philip Berrigan, Dorothy Day, Gordon Zahn, and other Catholic peace activists to be acknowledged as Catholic moralists. For them, it seems, a nuclear missile is an abomination. Sitting in its silo, deterring, it is the weapon of a bully, holding hostage the innocent lives of an adversary population. Once sent winging on its way, the horrible nature of the weapon is realized, not magically transformed from licit to illicit.

Furthermore, the claim that the church itself supports the wishy-washy deterrence-accepting policy of the American hierarchy, is not entirely correct. Certainly, the statements of the Vatican Council on this subject are something less than fully supportive of such a view, even though they were made at a time when no power held enough nuclear weapons to threaten the survival of the human race. The council did accept the fact that the accumulation of such arms does act "as a deterrent to possible enemy attack," and acknowledged the *fact* that "many regard this . . . as the most effective way in which peace of a sort can be maintained . . ." However, whatever be the case with this method of deterrence, the council denied that the resulting balance of terror provides "a sure and authentic peace." To the contrary, "The causes of war threaten to grow gradually stronger."

Rather than engage in the moral, logical, and semantic gymnastics needed to maintain its present neutral, lukewarm position, the American hierarchy would seem to be well advised to learn how to speak up, and act, on this matter, before it has to join the rest of us in a worldwide barbecue pit. In a truly moral response to the way things actually are, the bishops must somehow find the courage to denounce the weapons policies of both the Soviet Union and the United States. Such a denunciation could be fleshed out with specifics, including a demand that our government entirely replace its nuclear arsenal with conventional weapons.

The capacity of the American church to act courageously and issue more than fine words, when convinced that it is faced by a moral outrage, has been amply demonstrated by its response to the abortion issues. Accordingly we can expect that a growing awareness of the depravity inherent in the continued maintenance of our nuclear weapons system will finally provide the push needed to set similar corrective forces into motion. Certainly, neither the condemnation of specific weapons nor sanctions against their use is without precedent in the Catholic Church. At the time of the Second Lateran Council, the crossbow, a child's weapon by modern standards, was placed under interdict, as a barbarous weapon unfit for Christian warfare.

Although the basic responsibility for action against our own arsenals belongs to the American church, as people and institution, this response need not be limited to local options. Such actions can be intensified or new alternatives opened by calling on the resources of the universal church. For example, supportive sanctions such as the following might be issued from Rome.

Be it known that:

All persons knowingly involved in the launching of, or decision to use, either tactical or strategic nuclear weapons are excommunicated by the act of putting such weapons into use.

The day following the first use of atomic weapons by any major power, or by its satellites or allies, will be declared a holy day of obligation throughout the world. Requiem Masses will be offered for those killed at Hiroshima and Nagasaki and for all subsequent victims of nuclear warfare.

The citizens of all nations or coalitions of nations that employ atomic weapons, whether tactical or strategic, whether in first strike or in retaliation, will be required under pain of serious sin to begin seven days of penance for their share of our communal guilt. With limited exceptions, as determined by the local ordinary, this penance will include a complete abstention from all secular activity other than the minimum needed for the maintenance of life, health, and civil order.

The officials of nations that make first use of atomic weaponry are declared anathema. Such governments are judged to be outlaws, their laws are declared to be void, and their citizens are urged to set up responsible governments in their stead.

Nations that refrain from the use of atomic weapons in their response to armed aggression are considered to be fighting a just war, and should be supported by all lawful means.

The object of sanctions such as these would seem to be commendable: to lessen the suffering of mankind, to limit the loss of innocent life and to prevent foolish humans from transforming God's world into a radioactive cinder. As a matter of prudence, however, we have to ask whether these directives could accomplish what they seek, and whether they might cause more harm than good. They might be completely ineffective in punishing a nuclear aggressor and could be counterproductive, at worst.

Certainly, the argument that such sanctions would be ineffectual is reasonably persuasive. Most Roman Catholics are even less inclined now than in the past to listen to the church in matters that touch on what they see as their secular interests. In the United States the promulgation of such sanctions could be seen as a gross attempt to breach our constitutional separation of church and state. Enormous community pressure, backed by state police power, would be exerted against any such return to "medievalism."

These surely are valid arguments, yet they are undercut by the fact that the primary objective of the sanctions would be deterrence, not guaranteed effectiveness. Even though military planners might feel reasonably certain that such sanctions would have only marginal effects on a wartime effort, they could not be sure. In the United States they would be faced with the possibility, remote as it might seem, that with our first atomic salvo up to a quarter of the population might go on a week-long retreat (in effect, a general strike), or even rise in revolt. Of course, a peacetime Gallup poll would undoubtedly reassure such planners that their Roman Catholic populations would remain good Americans, good Germans, or whatever, in the war yet to come. However, the military could not help but be concerned that Christian consciences, functioning in the yet undetermined, unexperienced context of an incipient nuclear holocaust, might perceive their relation with eternity quite differently than they do now.

To an unpredictable and probably indeterminable extent, sanctions so strict as those listed would alienate large segments of our population, including many nominal Catholics. On the other hand, they could equally provide the basis for an ecumenical outreach. Men and women of all faiths, pacifists, and antinuclear activists might be encouraged to join in these sanctions or to develop appropriate sanctions of their own. A determined and united front such as this could well be enough to tip the perceived military cost-benefit balance toward a completely nonnuclear defense policy.

Much of the population of the United States and of other Western nations would, however, see such a result as playing into the hands of the communists. After all, the Soviet Union seems to be better prepared for conventional warfare than is the West, and it has far fewer Roman Catholics and professed Christians within its borders. On the other hand, the Soviets face not only the West, but China, Islam, and their own non-Russian populations as well. Furthermore, Lithuania and the Eastern bloc satellites bording the West are heavily Catholic in tradition at least. Indeed, the response of Poland's old-line Catholics to such sanctions could determine the success or failure of any invasion of, or from, the West.

This is just speculation, of course. All we really know is that action is needed and that opportunities for appropriate action exist. The exact form that such initiatives might take remains to be determined, but there is no doubt as to their objective, to head off an all-out nuclear war. To achieve this goal, any threatened antinuclear action must be substantial enough that it would favor the defeat of any nation foul and arrogant enough to make first use of atomic weapons. Secondly, it should give every possible advantage to any nation that restrained itself from responding in kind.

The sanctions of a church acting in what, frankly, must be seen as a pre-Vatican II mode, would seem to have some chance of success. The question is whether the price is too high. At least in the North American church, the promulgation of such sanctions would not likely reflect the will of the whole people of God, but would, rather, be seen as the arbitrary action of a rigid, autocratic hierarchy. Within the church as a whole, however, such an initiative might well be perceived in quite another way, as a necessary and appropriate response to an extremely grave situation. In times of war and crisis, even the most liberal of democracies revert to autocratic forms, just so they can survive.

The issue is survival. Whether we dare face it or not, the hands of the atomic clock are lurching toward midnight. We cannot just sit around, waiting for SALT III. With the help of the American churches we must make North America a nuclear-free zone.

Appendix C:

Glossary and Resources

Glossary
Key terms frequently used in a discussion of the arms race

This glossary has been designed to provide a reference to the acronyms, words, and phrases associated with the arms race and to clarify concepts and answer certain questions which arise in this context.

Atomic Bomb
A weapon whose energy is derived from the "fissioning" or splitting of the atom, releasing the radioactive elements of uranium and plutonium.

B-1 Bomber
A long-range intercontinental bomber designed to replace the fleet of 350 B-52 bombers as part of the Triad System. The bomber was tabled by the Carter Administration but is presently under active reconsideration.

Backfire
The NATO designation of the Soviet two-engine, swing-winged bomber. It is currently being deployed to operational units for use in a theater or naval strike role as a replacement for older Soviet medium bombers. Backfire has characteristics that fall between the characteristics generally attributed to existing heavy bombers and those of medium bombers. Under certain flight conditions, the Backfire is assessed by the United States to have an intercontinental capability. Restricting Soviet production of the Backfire bomber was a major element of the SALT II Treaty.

Counterforce
A nuclear war strategy (also referred to as "first strike capability") in which attack missiles are targeted against the opponent's military forces (airfields, missiles, naval facilities) rather than against cities as in the "Mutual Assured Destruction" (MAD) strategy. Since nuclear forces are virtually invulnerable once launched, the *counterforce* strategy presupposes the first use of nuclear weapons rather than a retaliatory strike. *(Note: The United States has never agreed to an international statement assuring that it would never be the first country to use nuclear weapons.)*

Cruise Missile
A guided missile that uses aerodynamic lift to offset gravity and propulsion to counteract drag. This weapon, able to be launched by aircraft, land-based, or ocean-going facilities, flies at treetop level undetectable by enemy radar. It can carry a nuclear warhead.

Deterrence
A nuclear war strategy (also known as "Balance of Terror") whereby a potential aggressor refrains from using nuclear weapons for fear of massive retaliation. The strategy has characterized the relations between the United States and the Soviet Union from the early 1950s until 1975 when the idea of *counterforce* was introduced.

Fallout
Radioactive debris produced by a nuclear explosion. This highly dangerous, cancer-causing material descends from the explosion to the surface of the earth, contaminating air, land, and water. It can be carried by the wind over great distances from the point of the initial blast.

Hydrogen Bomb
A thermonuclear weapon that generates its destructive power by a combination of atomic fusion and fission reactions. In contrast to the "fissioning" (or splitting) of atoms in the atomic bomb, the hydrogen bomb joins together (or "fuses") atomic nuclei.

Intercontinental Ballistic Missile (ICBM)
A land-based or mobile rocket-powered vehicle capable of delivering a warhead to intercontinental ranges. Once outside the atmosphere, ICBMs fly to a target on an elliptical trajectory. An ICBM consists of a booster, one or more reentry vehicles, and penetration aids. Today's ICBMs have an intercontinental range up to 4,000 miles and are capable of delivering a nuclear warhead with pinpoint accuracy.

Kiloton
A measure of the yield of a nuclear weapon equivalent to 1,000 tons of TNT. The bomb dropped on Hiroshima in World War II had an approximate yield of 12.5 kilotons.

Limited Nuclear War
The military strategy that presupposes that warring nations can or would limit the use of nuclear weapons to specific military or population centers. The strategy is based on the assumption that an exchange involving nuclear weapons would not quickly escalate into a full-scale war.

Megaton
A measure of the yield of a nuclear weapon equivalent to one million tons of TNT.

Multiple Reentry Vehicle (MRV)
The reentry vehicle of a ballistic missile equipped with multiple warheads where the missile cannot independently target each warhead.

Multiple Independently Targeted Reentry Vehicle (MIRV)
Multiple reentry vehicles carried by a ballistic missile, each of which can be directed to a separate and arbitrary location. A MIRV missile has a mechanism for targeting and firing each nuclear warhead to a specific location once it reenters the earth's atmosphere. One missile can therefore release a number of smaller missiles (each carrying a nuclear warhead) to destroy several cities or military targets.

Mutual Assured Destruction (MAD)
The nuclear war strategy that evolved between the United States and the Soviet Union since the early 1960s. It rests on the understanding that either side has the capacity to inflict massive destruction on the other in the event of a nuclear attack. This strategy, which maintains and enhances the deterrent effect between the superpowers, was in effect until 1975 when the *counterforce* or "first strike" strategy began to be discussed and implemented.

MX
The "missile experimental" or MX is a new, highly accurate missile mounted on special transports to make it mobile. The MX is supposed to augment current ICBMs and supposedly would be less vulnerable because it could be shuttled along special roadways and hidden in any number of garagelike protective structures.

National Security
A political and military term coined in the National Security Act of 1947. This act extended certain emergency powers to the President beyond those given in the Constitution. These powers included the perogative to suspend civil liberties under certain circumstances as well as to undertake covert, normally illegal actions (such as break-ins and wiretaps). Under this act, the United States has existed in an official state of national emergency since 1947. The development of nuclear weapons and the restriction of information about them have been accomplished largely without challenge because of the claims of national security.

Neutron Bomb
A radiation intensive weapon that can be delivered by missile or artillery shell. It is a miniature hydrogen bomb used against concentrations of tanks — by killing their crews with radiation. It has relatively little blast and heat effect on buildings and other civilian structures.

Overkill
The nuclear deterrent concept of having an ability to destroy the entire popula-

tion of an enemy several times over. Currently, the United States and the USSR possess a nuclear weapons capability which can destroy the earth's population fifteen times over.

Payload
Weapons and penetration aids carried by a delivery vehicle. In the case of missiles, the reentry vehicles and warheads are atop the main propulsion stages. In the case of strategic bombers, the bombs, missiles, or penetration aids are carried internally or attached to the wings or fuselage.

Plutonium
A radioactive, metallic element produced by the splitting of the uranium atom. Plutonium is used to make nuclear weapons and is produced by conventional nuclear power plants at the rate of several hundred pounds per plant each year. Only twenty pounds of plutonium is needed to produce an atomic bomb. *(Note: Plutonium is one of the most carcinogenic substances known and is so toxic that less than one-millionth of a gram can cause cancer. It retains its radioactivity and carcinogenic properties for almost 250,000 years.)*

Proliferation
The spread of nuclear weapons and nuclear materials to other nations largely as a result of the exportation of nuclear energy technology.

Strategic Arms Limitation Talks (SALT)
A series of negotiations between the United States and the Soviet Union that began in November 1969. SALT seeks to limit and reduce both offensive and defensive strategic arms. The first round of negotiations, known as SALT I, concluded in May 1972, resulted in two agreements — the ABM (Anti-Ballistic Missile) Treaty and the Interim Agreement on Certain Measures with Respect to the Limitation of Strategic Offensive Arms. SALT II, begun in November 1972, included a treaty, a protocol of shorter duration, and a Joint Statement of Principles and Basic Guidelines for Subsequent Negotiations on the Limitation of Strategic Arms. The SALT II treaty was signed by President Carter and Soviet President Brezhnev, offered for Senate ratification, then withdrawn following the Soviet invasion of Afghanistan in December 1979.

Strategic Nuclear Weapons
Long-range nuclear weapons with large kiloton or megaton yields carried on ICBMs, SLBMs, and intercontinental bombers.

Submarine-Launched Ballistic Missile (SLBM)
A rocket-propelled vehicle containing one or several nuclear warheads carried in, and launched from, a submarine.

Tactical Nuclear Weapon
Short-ranged weapons, such as the neutron bomb, intended for battlefield

operations, particularly in a limited nuclear war scenario. Most U.S. tactical nuclear weapons are deployed in Western Europe and South Korea.

Triad
The three-part combination of land-based ICBMs, airborne intercontinental bombers, and submarine-launched ballistic missiles (SLBMs) making up the deterrent forces of the United States and the USSR.

Trident Submarine and Trident I and II Missiles
The Trident is a nuclear-powered submarine longer than two football fields and five stories high. It is twice the size of the submarine it is intended to replace. The main difference between the Trident and other submarines is the greater number, power, and accuracy of its missiles.

Uranium
The heaviest element and basic raw material for nuclear power and nuclear weapons.

Warhead
That part of the missile, projectile, torpedo, rocket, or other munition that contains either the nuclear or thermonuclear system, the high-explosive system, the chemical or biological agents, or the inert materials intended to inflict damage.

Yield
The energy released in an explosion. The energy released in the detonation of a nuclear weapon is generally measured in terms of kilotons or megatons of TNT required to produce the same energy release.

Books

Aldridge, Robert J. *The Counterforce Syndrome: A Guide to U.S. Nuclear Weapons and Strategic Doctrine*. Washington, D.C.: Transnational Institute, 1978.

Aukerman, Dale. *Darkening Valley: A Biblical Perspective on Nuclear War*. New York: The Seabury Press, 1981.

Bainton, Ronald H. *Christian Attitudes Towards War and Peace*. Nashville: Abingdon Press, 1960.

Barnet, Richard J. *Roots of War*. Baltimore: Penguin Books, 1971.

_____ *The Giants: Russia and America*. New York: Simon & Schuster, 1977.

_____ *Real Security: Restoring American Power in a Dangerous Decade*. New York: Simon & Schuster, 1981.

Berrigan, Philip. *Of Beasts and Other Beastly Images: Essays Under the Bomb*. Portland, Ore.: Sunburst Press, 1978.

Boston Study Group. *The Price of Defense.* New York: Times Books, 1979.

Butterfield, H. *Christianity and History.* New York: Charles Scribner's Sons, 1950.

Caldicott, Helen. *Nuclear Madness: What You Can Do.* New York: Times Books, 1979.

Cooney, Robert and Michalowski, Helen (eds.). *The Power of the People: Active Nonviolence in the U.S.* Culver City, Calif.: Peace Press, 1977.

Del Vasto, Lanza. *Warriors of Peace.* New York: Alfred A. Knopf, 1974.

Donaghy, John and Osterle, William H. *Peace Theology and the Arms Race: Readings in Arms and Disarmament.* Philadelphia: College Theology Society Publications, 1980.

Douglas, James W. *The Non-Violent Cross: A Theology of Revolution & Peace.* New York: Macmillan, 1969.

_____ *Resistance and Contemplation: The Way of Liberation.* New York: Dell Publishing, 1972.

Durnbaugh, Donald F. (ed.) *On Earth Peace: Discussions on War/Peace Issues Between Friends, Mennonites, Brethren and European Churches 1935–1975.* Elgin, Ill: The Brethren Press, 1978.

Eller, Vernard. *King Jesus Manual of Arms for the Armless: War and Peace from Genesis to Revelation.* Nashville: Abingdon Press, 1973. Rev. ed. *War and Peace from Genesis to Revelation.* Scottdale, Pa.: Herald Press, 1981.

Ellul, Jacques. *Violence: Reflections from a Christian Perspective.* New York: The Seabury Press, 1969.

Fallows, James. *National Defense.* New York: Random House, 1981.

Ferguson, John. *The Politics of Love: The New Testament and Non-Violent Revolution.* Greenwood, S.C.: The Attic Press, 1976.

Gandhi, M. K. *Non-Violent Resistance.* New York: Schocken Books, 1967.

Grannis, J. Christopher, Laffin, Arthur J., and Schade, Elin. *The Risk of the Cross: Christian Discipleship in the Nuclear Age.* New York: The Seabury Press, 1981.

Gray, J. Glenn. *The Warriors: Reflections on Men in Battle.* New York: Harcourt, Brace and Company, 1959.

Guinan, Edward. *Peace and Nonviolence.* New York: Paulist Press, 1973.

Hachiya, Michihiko. *Hiroshima Diary.* Chapel Hill: The University of North Carolina Press, 1955.

Johansen, Robert C. *Toward a Dependable Peace: A Proposal for an Appropriate Security System.* New York: Institute for World Order, 1978.

Lasserre, Jean. *War and the Gospel.* Scottdale, Pa.: Herald Press, 1962.

Lens, Sidney. *The Day Before Doomsday: An Anatomy of the Nuclear Arms Race.* Boston: Beacon Press, 1977.

Lifton, Robert J. *Death in Life: Survivors of Hiroshima.* New York: Simon & Schuster, 1967.

Marcel, Gabriel. *Man Against Mass Society.* Chicago: Henry Regnery Company, 1952.

McSorley, Richard. *Kill? For Peace?* Washington, D.C.: Center for Peace Studies, Georgetown University, 1978.

_____ *New Testament Basis of Peacemaking.* Washington, D.C.: Center for Peace Studies, Georgetown University, 1979.

A Matter of Faith: A Study Guide for Churches on the Nuclear Arms Race. Washington, D.C.: *Sojourners* Magazine, 1981.

Melman, Seymour. *The Permanent War Economy.* New York: Simon & Schuster, 1974.

Merton, Thomas. *Faith and Violence.* Notre Dame, Ind.: University of Notre Dame Press, 1968.

Myrdal, Alva. *The Game of Disarmament: How the United States and Russia Run the Arms Race.* New York: Pantheon, 1978.

Rockman, Jane (ed.). *Peace in Search of Makers: Riverside Church Reverse the Arms Race Convocation.* Valley Forge, Pa.: Judson Press, 1979.

Sampson, Anthony. *The Arms Bazaar: From Lebanon to Lockheed.* New York: Bantam Books, 1973.

Sharp, Gene. *The Politics of Nonviolent Action.* Boston: Porter Sargent Publisher, 1973.

Shelly, Maynard, *New Call for Peacemakers: A New Call to Peacemaking Study Guide.* Newton, Ka.: Faith and Life Press, 1979.

Stringfellow, William. *An Ethic for Christians and Other Aliens in a Strange Land.* Waco, Tex.: Word Books Publisher, 1973.

_____ *Conscience and Obedience.* Waco, Tex.: World Books Publisher, 1977.

Trocmé, André. *Jesus and the Nonviolent Revolution.* Scottdale, Pa.: Herald Press, 1973.

Whynes, David K. *The Economics of Third World Military Expenditures.* Austin: University of Texas Press, 1979.

Yoder, John H. *The Politics of Jesus.* Grand Rapids, Mich.: Eerdmans, 1972.

Zahn, Gordon. *In Solitary Witness.* Boston: Beacon Press, 1964.

Articles

This compendium of articles on the arms race is not intended to be definitive. There have been literally thousands of articles written on this question over the last few years. This collection is merely intended to be a starting point for individual reading and research.

The Defense Budget and the Decision-Making Process

Stephen Chapman, "Santa at the Pentagon," *The New Republic,* December 29, 1979.

Lloyd J. Dumas, "Why Buying Guns Raises the Price of Butter," *Christianity and Crisis,* November 27, 1978.

John J. Fialka, "Rapid Deployment Force to Cost U.S. $10 Billion," *Washington Star,* December 15, 1979.

Lawrence J. Korb, "The Process and Problems of Linking Policy and Force Structure Through the Defense Budget Process," *Policy Studies Journal,* (Autumn 1979) 8,1, 92–98.

Richard Halloran, "Why Defense Costs So Much," *The New York Times,* January 11, 1981.

Guy Halverson, "U.S. Arms Buildup Reshaping Economy," *Christian Science Monitor,* February 8, 1980.

Joseph Kraft, "Defense Numbers Game," *Washington Post,* November 18, 1979.

Seymour Melman, "Looting the Means of Production," *The New York Times,* Sunday, July 26, 1981.

Merrill Sheils, "Politics of Arms Spending," *Newsweek,* June 22, 1981.

"Soviet 1980 Budget Cuts Military Outlay and Sets 8.8% Boost in Farm Production," *Wall Street Journal,* November 29, 1979.

Philip Taubman, "Arms Makers Seen Gaining Politically," *The New York Times,* June 16, 1981.

Joseph T. Vitale, "The Arms Race," *Episcopalian,* January 1981.

Tom Wicker, "4½ Percent for What?" *The New York Times,* December 16, 1979.

William F. Woo, "Are Carriers Worth Their Cost?" 2 pts., *St. Louis Post-Dispatch,* December 3 and 4, 1979.

Military Strategy and Security Matters

Martin Anderson, "Build Up the Reserves, Not Registration Lines," *Washington Post* (Outlook Section), Sunday, February 3, 1980.

"After Iran: Next Turn for U.S. Foreign Policy," *U.S. News and World Report,* December 31, 1979 (An interview with Zbigniew Brzezinski).

Richard J. Barnet, "Challenging the Myth of National Security," *The New York Times Magazine,* Sunday, April 1, 1979.

_____ , "The Myth of Power, The Power of Myth," *Christianity and Crisis,* November 27, 1978.

Warren Boroson and David P. Snyder, "the First Nuclear War," *Next,* October 1980.

Richard Burt, "Should U.S. Create a Quick-Strike Force?" *The New York Times,* December 1, 1979.

Arthur Macy Cox, "The CIA's Tragic Error," *New York Review of Books,* November 6, 1980.

Bernard T. Feld, "The Hands Move Closer to Midnight," *The Bulletin of the Atomic Scientists,* January 1980.

Gary Hart, "The Real Defense Issues," *Christian Science Monitor,* June 12, 1981.

"How a Nuclear War Could Start," *The Bulletin of the Atomic Scientists,* April 1979.

Miles Kahler, "Rumors of War: The 1914 Analogy," *Foreign Affairs,* 58, 2 (Winter 1979/1980), 374–396.

Irving Kristol, "The Worst is Yet to Come," *Wall Street Journal,* November 26, 1979.

Elizabeth Pond, "Deterring Nuclear War: The New Dangers," *Christian Science Monitor,* August 16, 1980.

———, "Deterring Nuclear War: The Long-Range Issues," *Christian Science Monitor,* August 28, 1980.

———, "Deterring Nuclear War: The Immediate Issues," *Christian Science Monitor,* August 29, 1980.

Stephen S. Rosenfeld, "Too Rapid Deployment," *Washington Star,* December 21, 1979.

Dr. Frederic Solomon and Dr. Mary Coleman, "Scientists Agree: No One Can Win a Nuclear War," *Miami Herald,* March 11, 1980.

George Sommaripa, "Measuring Power to Purpose: Toward a Rational Military Policy," *Christianity and Crisis,* May 26, 1980.

"U.S. Military Power — How It Can Be Used," *U.S. News and World Report,* December 3, 1979 (An interview with Stephen S. Kaplan).

Nuclear Weapons

Gordon Adams and David Gold, "Derail the MX," *The Nation,* November 10, 1979.

Robert C. Aldridge, "America Moves Closer to Nuclear War," *Los Angeles TImes,* December 7, 1979.

James J. Kilpatrick, "Nuclear Sanity and Goofy," *Washington Star,* November 20, 1979.

William H. Kincade, "Will MX Backfire?" *Foreign Policy,* No. 37, Winter 1979–80, 43–58.

"The New Defense Posture: Missiles, Missiles, and Missiles," *Business Week,* August 11, 1980.

Christopher E. Paine, "MX: The Public Works Project of the 1980s," *The Bulletin of the Atomic Scientists,* February, 1980.

Arms Sales

William Beecher, "Arms: A Strong Diplomatic Weapon," *Boston Globe,* November 23, 1979.

Paul Y. Hammond and David J. Louscher, "Growing Dilemmas for the Management of Arms Sales," *Armed Forces and Society,* 6,1 (Fall, 1979), 1–21.

Stanley Karnow, "U.S. Arms Sales: A Failed Policy," *Baltimore Sun,* December 17, 1979.

"The Scramble to Cash in on Weapons Exports," *Business Week,* March 24, 1980.

Robert R. Ulin, "The Weapons Connection," *Military Review,* November 1979, 55–65.

Arms Control and Salt

Omar Bradley, "This Ultimate Threat," *The New York Times,* April 10, 1981.

McGeorge Bundy, "Strategic Deterrence After Thirty Years: What Has Changed?" *Survival,* 21:5, September/October 1979.

Walter Clemens, Jr., "How the Russians Look at SALT," *Worldview,* September 1979.

Richard Falk, "Security Begins at Home," *The Nation,* October 29, 1979.

"The Future of Arms Control," *Foreign Policy,* No. 36, Fall 1979, 20–48.

Sidney Lens and George Ott, "The Wrong Debate," *The Progressive,* October 1979.

Brad Knickerbocker, "Dirty A-Bomb Easy to Build, Article Warns," *Christian Science Monitor,* December 3, 1979.

Elizabeth Pond, "Deterring Nuclear War: The Soviet View," *Christian Science Monitor,* August 27, 1980.

Peacemaking, Stewardship, and Christian Responsibility

Tom Buckley, "A Voice of Reason Among the Nuclear Warriors," *Quest/81,* March 1981.

William Sloane Coffin, Jr., "Dealing with the Devil: A Cost-Benefit Analysis," *Christianity and Crisis,* November 27, 1978.

Robert Culver, "Between War and Peace: Old Debate in a New Age," *Christianity Today,* October 24, 1980.

Eileen Egan, "Christian Pacifism" *The Catholic Worker,* February, 1980.

George Kennan, "The Only Way Out of the Nuclear Nightmare is by a Bold and Sweeping Gesture," *Manchester Guardian,* May 25, 1981.

Edward LeRoy Long, Jr., "What Makes a War Just," *Christian Science Monitor,* February 10, 1981.

Earl Louis Mountbatten, "A Statement on War," *The Defense Monitor,* May 1980.

Allan M. Parrent, "To Pray and Work for Peace: The Episcopal Church and the Peace Issue," *Virginia Seminary Journal,* July 1980.

Jerry Richardson, "The Outlook for Peace," *The Futurist,* December 1978.

Glen Stassen, "Petitioning God for Peace," *Sojourners,* April 1981.

Richard G. Watts, "Peacemaking in the Parishes," *The Christian Century,* April 8, 1981.

William F. Wolff, "The Church and the Bomb," *America,* January 10, 1981.

Audiovisual Resources*

"Atomic Age: A Trail of Victims"   A 20-minute slide presentation on the plight of people who have been exposed to radiation from nuclear technology. Fellowship of Reconciliation, Box 271, Nyack, NY 10960.

"Conscience and War Taxes"   A 20-minute slide show on the conscientious opposition to taxes used for war and military purposes. National Council for a World Peace Tax Fund, 2111 Florida Ave. NW, Washington, DC 20008.

"Ground Zero at Bangor"   A 26-minute, 16 mm color film, focusing on the issues of unilateral disarmament and military superiority. Religious Broadcasting Commission, 356 Post-Intelligence Bldg., 521 Wall Street, Seattle, WA 98121.

"Hiroshima/Nagasaki"   Films depicting the 1945 atomic destruction of these two Japanese cities. Wilmington College, Wilmington, OH 45177.

"Last Slide Show"   Traces military history to the present nuclear threat and promotes the goals of the Mobilization for Survival.

"Mr. Nixon's Secret Legacy"   A 30-minute film produced by the BBC in 1974 on U.S. "counterforce" capability as well as a series of interviews with people who are prepared to comply with orders to unleash nuclear weapons. Mennonite Central Committee, 21 S. 12 St., Akron, PA 17501.

"Paul Jacobs and the Nuclear Gang"   A film about how civilians and soldiers were exposed to the atomic tests of the 1950s with a particular focus on Paul Jacobs, a journalist, who after a long illness of leukemia, died in 1978. Film Donnelly/Colt, Box 271, New Vernon, NJ 07976.

"Thinking Twice"   A 30-minute documentary about an American family facing the harsh realities of the nuclear arms race and its personal implications on their lives. SKYE Pictures, Inc., 1460 Church St. NW, Washington, DC 20005.

"War Without Winners" A 30-minute film on the need to reverse the arms race from an American and a Soviet perspective. Produced by the Center for Defense Information. Available from the CDI on Films, Inc., 733 Green Bay Road, Wilmette, IL 60091.

*Additional listings of audiovisual aids are available from various groups listed below. These are identified with the code: **A**.

Two extensive film guides are:

Films, Videotapes, and Slideshows Update
A guide listing 70 films and slideshows which address a broad range of nuclear issues. (50¢) Nuclear Information and Resource Service, 1526 16th St. NW, Washington, DC 20036.

War, Peace Film Guide by John Dowling
187 pages of films (annotated), organizations, and viewing suggestions. ($5.00) World Without War Publications, 67 E. Madison, Suite 1417, Chicago, IL 60603.

Domestic Organizations and Groups Working on the National and Local Level for Peace, Disarmament and Social Justice.*

AMERICAN COMMITTEE ON EAST-WEST ACCORD
An educational organization aimed at improving East-West relations. Publishes "Common Sense in U.S.-Soviet Relations," and a film, "Survival or Suicide." **L,A,S**
For information contact: American Committee on East-West Accord, 227 Massachusetts Avenue NE, #300, Washington, DC 20002. (202) 546-1700

AMERICAN FRIENDS SERVICE COMMITTEE (AFSC)
Advances nonviolent action for change. Works to build informed resistance to war and militarism. Activities stress programs on conversion and dependency on defense spending. Publishes a wide variety of resources on peace and disarmament. **L,A,S,C**
For information contact: American Friends Service Committee (AFSC), 1501 Cherry Street, Philadelphia, PA 19102. (215) 241-7177

ARMS CONTROL AND DISARMAMENT AGENCY
Publications include materials on previous disarmament treaties, U.S.-USSR relations, nonproliferation, the SALT Treaty, comprehensive test ban, etc. The Department of State, Bureau of Public Affairs, Washington, DC 20520, also produces a wide variety of material on U.S. government positions on various foreign and military policies. Publishes a monthly two-page sheet, "Gist." **L**

*See code on page 138.

For information contact: The Arms Control and Disarmament Agency, Department of State, Washington, DC 20451. (202) 632-3597

ARMS CONTROL ASSOCIATION
A nonpartisan national membership organization dedicated to promoting public understanding of effective policies for arms control, security, and disarmament. Publishes a regular newsletter "Arms Control Today." **L,S,C**
For information contact: Arms Control Association, 11 Dupont Circle NW, Washington DC 20036. (202) 797-6450

THE CATHOLIC WORKER
The oldest of the more than fifty existing Catholic Worker communities in the United States that is committed to the "works of mercy and peace" from a Gospel-pacifist perspective. Publishes a monthly newspaper. **L,S**
For information contact: The Catholic Worker, 36 E. First Street, New York, NY 10012. (212) 254-1640

CENTER ON LAW AND PACIFISM
Focuses on legal counseling for war tax resistance and provides information on conscientious objection in the nuclear age. **L,S**
For information contact: Center on Law and Pacifism, Box 1584, Colorado Springs, CO 80901. (303) 635-0041

CENTER FOR DEFENSE INFORMATION (CDI)
Conducts extensive research and public education on U.S. military policies. Publishes monthly newsletter called "Defense Monitor." **L,A,S**
For information contact: Center for Defense Information (CDI), 122 Maryland Avenue NE, Washington, DC 20002. (202) 543-0400

THE CHURCHES' CENTER FOR THEOLOGY AND PUBLIC POLICY
An ecumenical study center whose purpose is to strengthen the vocations of Christian leadership in the political order. **L,S,C**
For information contact: The Churches' Center for Theology and Public Policy, 4400 Massachusetts Avenue NW, Washington, DC 20016. (202) 363-3088

CLERGY AND LAITY CONCERNED (CALC)
An interfaith organization dedicated to religious political action for justice and peace. Distributes a 24-page guide, "Worship and Action Resources for a Non-Nuclear Future." Offers a wide range of other disarmament resources. **L,A,S,C**
For information contact: Clergy and Laity Concerned (CALC), 198 Broadway, New York, NY 10038. (212) 964-6730

COALITION FOR A NEW FOREIGN AND MILITARY POLICY
Unites forty-three national religious, labor, peace, research, and social-action

organizations working for a peaceful, noninterventionist and demilitarized U.S. foreign policy. Distributes a varity of disarmament resources. **L,A,S,C**
For information contact: Coalition for a New Foreign and Military Policy, 120 Maryland Avenue NE, Washington, DC 20002. (202) 546-8400

COMMITTEE AGAINST REGISTRATION AND THE DRAFT
A coalition of organizations to block reinstitution of conscription efforts in peace time. Local organizing is currently in progress. **L,S**
For information contact: Committee Against Registration and the Draft, 201 Massachusetts Avenue NE, Washington, DC 20002. (202) 547-4340

COUNCIL ON ECONOMIC PRIORITIES, CONVERSION INFORMATION CENTER
An organization established to respond to inquiries from other organizations seeking information on defense dependency and conversion. The Conversion Information Center produces regular data reports for use in national and local efforts. **L,S**
For information contact: The Council on Economic Priorities, Conversion Information Center, 84 Fifth Avenue, New York, NY 10011. (212) 691-8550

COVENANT PEACE COMMUNITY
A Gospel-based community in Connecticut working for nuclear disarmament and social justice. Affiliated with Atlantic Life Community. **L,A,S,C**
For information contact: Covenant Peace Community, 66 Edgewood Ave., New Haven, CT 06511. (203) 562-7935

THE EPISCOPAL PEACE FELLOWSHIP (EPF)
An independent society of Episcopalians working for reconciliation between people and nations, and pledged to renounce participation in war as far as possible. **L,S**
For information contact: The Reverend Denise Giardina, The Episcopal Peace Fellowship, Hearst Hall (Room 232), Wisconsin Avenue and Woodley Road NW, Washington, DC 20016. (202) 363-5532

FEDERATION OF AMERICAN SCIENTISTS
A lobbying organization composed of 6,000 scientists concerned with the use of science in society, especially the development of weapons of mass destruction. They produce books and reports on a full range of arms control and disarmament issues. **L**
For information contact: Federation of American Scientists, 307 Massachusetts Avenue, NE, Washington, DC 20002. (202) 546-3300

FELLOWSHIP OF RECONCILIATION
Makes parish resources available for studying and addressing the arms race question. Of particular emphasis is nuclear weapons control. Has many local and denominational fellowships. Publishes *Fellowship,* a monthly magazine. **L,S,A**

For information contact: Dan Ebener, Fellowship of Reconciliation, Box 271, Nyack, NY 10906. (914) 358-4601

GLOBAL EDUCATION ASSOCIATES
An interfaith education organization working nationally and internationally for world justice. Publishes a variety of curricular resources for schools and study groups on justice and peace issues. L,S,C
For information contact: Global Education Associates, 522 Park Avenue, East Orange, NJ 07117. (201) 675-1409

GROUND ZERO: CENTER FOR NONVIOLENT ACTION
The organizing base for the nonviolent campaign to halt construction of the Trident submarine base which is being built in the Puget Sound area of Bangor, Washington.
For information contact: Ground Zero: Center for Nonviolent Action, Rt. 5, Box 5423, Poulsbo, WA 98370.

INSTITUTE FOR DEFENSE AND DISARMAMENT STUDIES (IDDS)
A research and public education center studying the nature and purposes of military forces. Publishes the *American Peace Directory* which includes 2,000 national and local peace groups. L,S
For information contact: The Institute for Defense and Disarmament Studies (IDDS), 251 Harvard Street, Brookline, MA 02146. (617) 734-4216

INSTITUTE FOR POLICY STUDIES
A research and public education organization concerned with international issues including disarmament. Publishes books and other materials on disarmament. L,A,C
For information contact: The Institute for Policy Studies (IPS), 901 Q Street NW, Washington, DC 20009. (202) 234-9382

INSTITUTE FOR WORLD ORDER
Produces written and audiovisual resources on the arms race. L,A,S,C
For information contact: The Institute for World Order, 777 United Nations Plaza, New York, NY 10017. (212) 490-0010

INTERNATIONAL ASSOCIATION OF MACHINISTS
An international union supporting planned economic conversion to a "peace" economy. Has produced the recent study "The Impact of Military Spending on the Machinist's Union," and the newsletter "The Machinist." L
For information contact: The International Association of Machinists, 1300 Connecticut Avenue NW, Washington, DC 20036.

JONAH HOUSE
A Gospel-based community committed to nonviolent resistance against the nuclear arms race. Contact for the Atlantic Life Community, which is a

network of East Coast resistance communities involved in nonviolent campaigns at the Pentagon, White House, and nuclear weapons facilities. Publishes a regular newsletter called "Year One."
For information contact: Jonah House, 1933 Park Avenue, Baltimore, MD 21217.

MILITARISM AND EDUCATION PROGRAM OF UNITED MINISTRIES IN EDUCATION

Strives to embody the church's commitment to global peace by challenging higher education to utilize its teaching, research, and publication resources for the development of constructive and nonmilitary models of conflict resolution. Confronts our dependence on military solutions for national and global problems. Has published a number of resources on militarism and education. **L,A,S,C**
For information contact: Militarism and Education Program of United Ministries in Education, 1451 Dundee Avenue, Elgin, IL 60120. (312) 742-5100.

MOBILIZATION FOR SURVIVAL (MFS)

A coalition of groups that emphasize grassroots organization and action toward reversing the arms race and halting nuclear power plants. The Religious Task Force of the MFS is actively involved in organizing around the same goals. It is a clearinghouse for an array of antinuclear resources including an audiovisual guide. **L,A,S**
For information contact: Mobilization for Survival (MFS), 3601 Locust Walk, Philadelphia, PA 19104. (215) 386-4875

NATIONAL ACTION/RESEARCH ON THE MILITARY-INDUSTRIAL COMPLEX (NARMIC)

A project of the American Friends Service Committee (AFSC) that provides educational resources on U.S. foreign policy and local military contracting including "Arming for the 80s," a series of military-industrial maps and "How to Research Your Local War Industry."
For information contact: National Action/Research on the Military-Industrial Complex (NARMIC), 1501 Cherry Street, Philadelphia, PA 19102.

NATIONAL CITIZENS' HEARINGS FOR RADIATION VICTIMS

An organization that focuses on radiation hazards related to the nuclear industry. Offers slide shows and other resources on radiation.
For information contact: National Citizens' Hearings for Radiation Victims, 317 Pennsylvania Ave., SE, Washington, DC 20003.

NATIONAL COUNCIL OF CHURCHES OF CHRIST IN THE U.S.A.

A national council of major Protestant and Orthodox denominations. Publishes a statement, "To Preserve and Not Destroy: Statements on Disarmament." **L**

For information contact: National Council of Churches of Christ in the U.S.A., 475 Riverside Drive, New York, NY 10115. (212) 870-2286

NATIONAL INTERRELIGIOUS SERVICE BOARD FOR CONSCIENTIOUS OBJECTION (NISBCO)

A coalition of religious groups that oppose all forms of registration, the draft, or compulsory national service. Provides resources on countering military recruiting and on draft counseling, including a booklet on religious statements on conscientious objection. **L**

For information contact: The National Interreligious Service Board for Conscientious Objection (NISBCO), 550 Washington Building, 15th and New York Avenue NW, Washington, DC 20005. (202) 393-4868

NETWORK

A Catholic, multi-issue social justice lobby. Publishes quarterly articles on SALT and disarmament, including Vatican statements on this question. **L**

For information contact: Network, 806 Rhode Island Avenue NE, Washington, DC 20018. (202) 526-4070

PACIFIC LIFE COMMUNITY

A network of West Coast resistance communities involved in a nonviolent campaign to stop the Trident program. PLC is helping to build a transnational community of nonviolent resistance against nuclear weapons with peoples of the Pacific. Ground Zero is another contact for this group. Publishes a regular newsletter.

For information contact: Pacific Life Community, 631 Kiely Boulevard, Santa Clara, CA 95051.

PACIFIC STUDIES CENTER

Publishes "Pacific Research," which focuses on U.S. foreign and military policies, multinational corporations, and the political economy of Asia and the Pacific. Extensive library available to researchers. **L,S**

For information contact: Pacific Studies Center, 867 W. Dana Street, #204, Mountain View, CA 94041. (415) 969-1545

PAX CHRISTI

A national Catholic pacifist organization involved in acting for and educating about peacemaking and nuclear disarmament. Distributes Catholic-oriented resources on peace and disarmament. **L,A,S,C**

For information contact: Pax Christi, 3000 North Mango Avenue, Chicago, IL 60634. (312) 637-2555

PHYSICIANS FOR SOCIAL RESPONSIBILITY (PSR)

A group of health and medical professionals that provide information about the health hazards of nuclear weaponry and nuclear power. **L,A,S**

For information contact: Physicians for Social Responsibility (PSR), Box 295, Cambridge, MA 02236. (617) 924-3468

RIVERSIDE CHURCH DISARMAMENT PROGRAM

Provides speakers and resources for local disarmament education. Published book, *Peace in Search of Makers*. Distributes a religious slideshow on disarmament and publishes a regular newsletter. **L,A,S,C**
For information contact: Riverside Church Disarmament Program, 490 Riverside Drive, New York, NY 10027. (212) 222-5900 Ext. 237 or 238

ROCKY FLATS/NUCLEAR WEAPONS FACILITIES PROJECT (FOR/AFSC)

Information on projects around the country, especially Rocky Flats Nuclear Facility, that organize action to convert local nuclear weapons facilities to socially useful production. Distributes an organizing packet.
For information contact: Rocky Flats/Nuclear Weapons Facilities Project (FOR/AFSC), 1428 Lafayette Street, Denver, CO 80218.

SANE

Mobilizes grassroots initiatives for peace and disarmament, with emphasis on planned economic conversion. Publishes "The Conversion Planner." Also distributes a newsletter and other resources. **L,A,S,C**
For information contact: SANE, 514 C Street NE, Washington, DC 20002. (202) 546-7100

SOJOURNERS

A Christian evangelical community working for church renewal, social justice, and nuclear disarmament. Publishes a monthly magazine, peace ministries for religious-oriented disarmament resources, and a new book on the nuclear arms race and the religious community. **L,S,C**
For information contact: *Sojourners,* 1309 L Street NW, Washington, DC 20005. (202) 737-2780

U.S. CATHOLIC CONFERENCE

Addresses the issues of the arms race within the context of church teachings. Distributes materials on this subject. **L.S**
For information contact: U.S. Catholic Conference/Office of International Justice and Peace, 1312 Massachusetts Ave. NW, Washington, DC 20005. (202) 659-6600

WAR RESISTERS LEAGUE (WRL)

A national pacifist group that opposes armaments, conscription, and war; it relates the problem of war to economic and social justice. Publishes "WRL News" bimonthly and *WIN* magazine. **L,A,S**
For information contact: War Resisters League (WRL), 339 Lafayette Street, New York, NY 10012. (212) 228-0450

WOMEN'S INTERNATIONAL LEAGUE FOR PEACE AND FREEDOM (WILPF)

An international organization that emphasizes nonviolent solutions to domestic and international problems. Works actively on disarmament. Publishes "Peace and Freedom Newsletters" and other resources. **L,A,S,C** For information contact: Women's International League for Peace and Freedom (WILPF), 1213 Race Street, Philadelphia, PA 19107. (215) 563-7110.

WOMEN'S STRIKE FOR PEACE (WSP)
A group of women dedicated to achieving international disarmament under effective controls. They work to ban nuclear testing and to end the arms race. Publishes newsletter, leaflets, and action alerts. For information contact: Women's Strike for Peace (WSP), 145 South 13 Street, Philadelphia, PA 19107.

WORLD PEACEMAKERS
A religious-political group working for world peace. Publishes "World Peace" papers and "Handbook for World Peacemaker Groups." **L,S** For information contact: World Peacemakers, 2852 Ontario Road NW, Washington, DC 20009. (202) 265-7582

WORLD WITHOUT WAR
A resource center for longer-range peace education for religious institutions. Has developed religious curricula on religion and peace, resources on nonviolent resolutions of conflicts, and guidelines for writers and editors in peace studies. **L,A,C** For information contact: World Without War, 175 Fifth Avenue, New York, NY 10010. (212) 674-2085

CODES

L = Literature (brochures, books, booklets, pamphlets, etc.) available

S = Speakers available through organization

A = Audiovisual material (films, slide presentations, etc.) available

C = Curricular material available